KT-451-830

Fish

COMPETITION
TRAINING
FOR HORSE AND RIDER

TO11496   24,29

Accession Number.........................

Class Number.........636.14

MONTY MORTIMER

COMPETITION TRAINING

FOR HORSE AND RIDER

David & Charles

I am very grateful to Caroline Appelbe for so generously allowing me to use her charming, and most accurate, sketches of the Badminton Horse Trials cross-country fences to illustrate this book.

All photographs taken by the author except pages 6 and 98 (below) Kit Houghton and page 45 by Bob Langrish

A DAVID & CHARLES BOOK

Copyright © Monty Mortimer 1993, 1996
First published 1993
Published in paperback 1996

Monty Mortimer has asserted his right to be identified as author of this work in accordance with the Copyright, Designs and Patents Act 1988.

All rights reserved. No part of this publication may be reproduced, stored in a retrieval system, or transmitted, in any form or by any means, electronic, mechanical, by photocopying, recording or otherwise, without prior permission in writing from the publisher.

A catalogue record for this book is available from the British Library.

ISBN 0 7153 9961 6 (hardback)
ISBN 0 7153 0473 9 (paperback)

Typeset in Century Old Style 10.5/12.5
by ABM Typographics Ltd, Hull
and printed in Italy by Milanostampa SpA
for David & Charles
Brunel House   Newton Abbot   Devon

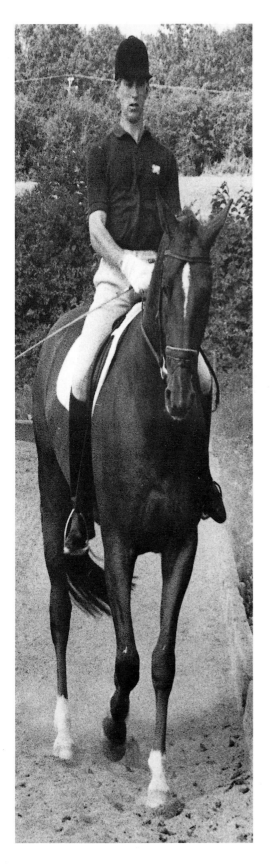

CONTENTS

INTRODUCTION

In a discussion on training horses and riders, in fact in any discussion involving the horse, the only 'generalisation' that it is safe to make is that 'all generalisations may be at the best unhelpful and at the worst misleading'. But the horse world is full of generalisations which have been developed over the past 3,000 years, in fact since Man first began to record his thoughts on the horse.

The basic rules for training both horses and riders have been distilled over the centuries from the opinions of intellectual horsemen who have had the education and experience to be able to record their views for posterity. It is from these views, with the exclusion of some of the more esoteric opinions, that modern principles have been established. Much of what has been written is clearly common sense, but this 'common sense' is not always obvious until the relevant problems and pitfalls have been experienced.

Part of the fascination of training horses is that no two animals are identical. They vary in conformation, intelligence, temperament, courage, athletic ability, adaptability and in many other qualities, all of which affect their ability to be trained. It is this wide variation in their qualities that beggars any one set of rules, or school of thought, being recommended for the training of all horses.

However, the trainer must have a clear start-line and some basic principles on which to establish his work, and this book examines these.

The successful trainer will study the views of those who have gone before him, and the techniques of his contemporaries. Only by being open-minded and observant will he be able to employ those techniques that are productive and helpful and discard those that are unrewarding, or in some cases, dangerous. It is sometimes said, of training horses, that 'many roads lead to Rome'. This is clearly so, but deviations in the form of short-cuts often create problems that are difficult, if not impossible to rectify. An important technique that sucessful trainers develop is that of employing exercises and equipment that improve the horse's balance, suppleness, agility, co-ordination, athletic ability, strength, stamina, and understanding of what the trainer requires *without causing problems at a later stage of training*. It is with this in mind that the more esoteric principles of horse training should be considered with care and circumspection.

The more simple and straightforward the work can be kept, the more the chances of success are enhanced and the risks of failure and disappointment reduced.

ONE

SELECTING THE POTENTIAL COMPETITION HORSE

Size	8	Breeding	10
Type	8	Conformation	10
Sex	8	Blemishes	19
Performance	9		

SIZE

Broadly speaking, large horses are stronger than small ones, though they are not necessarily faster, nor do they have more stamina. The size of the horse selected as a potential competition horse depends on a number of factors:

1. The rules relating to the horse's height, and whether or not ponies can compete in the in the same classes as horses, varies between the equestrian disciplines. In showjumping, ponies can compete with horses provided that they are registered as horses. In horse trials, horses must be 15 hands (152cm) high. Therefore the competition for which the horse is being selected influences the choice from a height point of view.

2. The horse must be big enough to carry the rider, but not so big and strong that a small, lightweight rider will have difficulty riding him. It is never flattering for a rider to look 'under-horsed'.

3. Whilst some small horses are very agile, mobile and fast, in disciplines where the horse is required to gallop long distances and jump high, solid fences with wide spreads, a big, strong animal of some substance is clearly an advantage. Major horse trials and show-jumping championships have been won by very small horses and ponies, but they are the exception rather than the rule.

TYPE

Many different 'types' of horse are found, but a 'type' is not a breed. For example, the 'hunter type' is usually a good, general-purpose competition horse. He will probably have a certain amount of Thoroughbred blood with perhaps some Irish Draught, Connemara or heavy horse blood. The result of this sort of cross is a tough, sound horse with a good, reasonably equable temperament that can gallop and jump with speed and stamina.

The cob is a type popular as a weight carrier. Cobs are very strong and of placid nature, and sometimes make good showjumpers; however, their limited galloping ability restricts their usefulness as event horses, and their paces are not usually of the quality that appeals to the dressage judge.

Pony 'types' are often fast, and good jumpers, and are generally good all-rounders up to a surprisingly high level. Their weight-carrying ability may be limited, however, under demanding competition conditions.

SEX

The truly outstanding horse may be a mare, a gelding or a stallion.

As regards stallions, the qualities of Thoroughbred stallions (speed, courage) are currently most sought after by the flat-racing industry, where breeding potential is an important consideration; a stallion is also suited to dressage, where his courage, and the more powerful movement, presence and elegance of an entire are invaluable. And

● **Fig 1** A fine type of competition horse for any discipline. This young horse shows sound conformation, has a good 'outlook' and athletic appearance

stallions are increasingly being proved successful showjumpers, although they can be difficult in company with mares and geldings in the close proximity of the collecting ring or other competition circumstances; however, this does depend on their personality.

Mares come into season approximately every month for four or five days from about February until August/September; during this period some mares lose their concentration, and may not, therefore, be at their best as competitors.

For average, steady reliability the gelding can probably be proved to be the most reliable choice.

PERFORMANCE

When selecting a competition horse for a rider, a major consideration is the animal's stage of training and its record of past performance. It is usually a mistake for a young, untrained horse to be paired with a very novice rider; many potentially good horses are spoilt in this way. It is equally unsatisfactory for a really novice rider to be matched with an advanced horse – the possibilities for accident and disappointment here are many. Ideally a 'schoolmaster' (a reliable horse with a certain amount of experience) should be found for the novice rider who is trying to gain experience. These are valuable horses, and very much sought after.

In an ideal world, all young horses would be trained by experienced riders who would eventually pass them on to train novice riders. However, this situation is hardly likely to be realised, and trainers will continue to be faced with novice riders on untrained horses. However, under skilled supervision a novice rider can learn a great deal by training a young horse or retraining a spoilt horse.

BREEDING

Generalisations on this subject can be misleading, and good competition horses of diverse breed and cross-breeding are found in all equestrian disciplines. However, there are often certain basic qualities, found in certain particular breeds, that make these more or less suitable for particular horse sports. For example, in diciplines where the horse is required to gallop fast – horse trials or point-to-pointing – Thoroughbred blood is required; in dressage, where elegance, strength and a steady temperament are required, the continental warmbloods are at an advantage; and the stamina and toughness of the Arab make him a good long-distance horse. The influence of some pony breeding often produces desirable qualities in the competition horse: for example the extravagant paces of the Welsh Cob can be of value in the dressage horse, and those tough, agile Argentinian ponies make very good polo ponies. The Spanish Riding School of Vienna works exclusively with the Lippizana, as this breed has all the qualities the school needs to perform its particular type of dressage including the airs above the ground. The Cadre Noir at Saumur chooses the Anglo Arab, as he is better suited to their requirements of greater speed, elegance and extreme athleticism.

CONFORMATION

The well conformed horse, in any discipline, should give an appearance of balanced elegance. In some disciplines, showing for instance, this is a requirement of the highest importance; in others, jumping and racing for example, conformational faults are only relevant if they impair the animal's training or performance. The significance of conformational faults in the competition horse is twofold:

1 | The faults may prevent him from being physically able to carry out the task required eg insufficient heart- and lung-room in the chest cavity may prevent him from being able to gallop fast for long distances.

2 | The faults may mean that the part in question is not able to withstand the rigours of training, and that the horse will break down: for example, a shoulder or pasterns which are too upright, or boxy feet, may be unable to absorb the constant concussion of training, and this could lead to any of the concussion-related conditions e.g. pedal ostitis, ringbone, navicular disease.

● **Fig 2** A Thoroughbred mare and her well-grown foal in ideal surroundings. Care at this level reaps its reward in the mature horse

• **Fig 3** A compact, well conformed, muscular horse, working well at elementary level

These theories are sometimes confounded by the fact that some highly successful, champion horses can be seen to have major conformational faults which nevertheless do not appear to have impaired their progress in any way. Horses that have been refused a Certificate of Soundness by the veterinary surgeon because they have failed the spavin test for instance, have competed successfully at international level in combined training.

The perfectly conformed horse is a rare creature; and since most potential competitors looking for a horse are to some degree restricted financially, this inevitably means they have to accept something less than perfect in their selection.

The purpose of this discussion is to identify:

1 | Those faults in conformation that should be avoided at all costs.
2 | Those which, with care, the trainer can make allowances for in the horse's training programme, and which good stable management can alleviate, in order that the horse may still be trained to be a useful competitor.

It is tempting, when assessing a horse's conformation, to look first at his head; but whilst this is important, it is not the most important factor: the overall picture is the first consideration. The questions to be asked in this respect are:

1 | Is the overall impression that he is all one horse, or does he appear to be made up from unrelated spare parts?
2 | Does the hind-quarter appear to be noticeably larger/smaller than the fore-quarter?
3 | Does he appear to be too high for his length, or too long for his height?
4 | Does he appear to slope up- or downhill? Is the point of croup higher than the wither?
5 | Is his appearance of athletic elegance, or is he dull and inelegant?
6 | Is his overall appearance one of substance and strength, or general weakness?

11

The head

The conformation of the head is important for several reasons, first of all because it plays an important part in locomotion – it is used as a balancing weight as the horse walks, canters and gallops, and also plays some part in his balance at trot. Any inability to swing the head and neck in an up-and-down movement in gallop may reduce the efficiency of the gallop by up to 10 per cent. A head that is too big and heavy may therefore impede the horse's balance.

The conformation of the jaw may affect the efficient utilisation of food. The lips, incisor teeth and molar teeth start the digestion of food; if the mouth is 'overshot' (the incisors of the upper jaw overlapping those of the lower jaw) or 'undershot' (the incisors of the lower jaw overlapping those of the upper jaw) the animal may have difficulty in grazing or taking food from the manager. These deformities of the incisor teeth may lead to 'quidding', when half-chewed food drops from the mouth while the horse is masticating it; this is both wasteful and detrimental to the horse, who may not hold his condition when in training.

The width of the jaw, across the bars of the

mouth, is important in respect of bit-fitting. A jaw that is too wide or too narrow may cause problems when selecting a bit.

Some horses have a low soft palate which may result in the joint of a jointed bit touching the roof of the mouth (particularly when used with a noseband fitted below the bit), which is undesirable. Also an over-large or thick tongue may cause problems, especially when fitting a double bridle.

The way in which the head joins the neck is important, too: there must be sufficient substance so that the neck appears to carry the head with ease, but the distance through that joint should not be so thick that it restricts flexion of the head on the neck. If the joint between the head and neck is too narrow (sometimes described as being 'cock-throttled'), the space through which air passes to the lungs and food to the stomach may be restricted, which is a disadvantage.

Large nostrils facilitate good passage of air to the lungs; small nostrils restrict it.

Good breadth between the eyes is desirable: the more the eyes are set towards the side of the head, the better the peripheral vision.

The neck

The conformation of the neck is important because it carries the head and plays a major part in locomotion and balance. A neck that is too long and thin is not only inelegant, it is also unlikely to be strong enough to carry the head either efficiently (at speed, or when jumping), or with 'presence'. Where the neck is too short – 'bull-necked' – the horse is often strong, and can set his jaw against his rider by putting his chin on his chest.

Another fault is the 'ewe' neck, where the crest (between the poll and the withers) is concave rather than convex; this invariably creates difficulties when attempting to teach the horse to relax in the neck, the poll and the jaw, and to come onto the bit. There is also the 'swan' neck, where the concave area is at the lower end of the neck, just in front of the wither.

The wither

The main requirement of the wither is that it should be sufficiently prominent for a saddle to fit well without slipping forward, but not so prominent that it makes it difficult to find a saddle with a front arch high enough to clear it.

● **Fig 4** A good head, large enough without being coarse, and well set onto the neck. Note the bright eye and large nostril

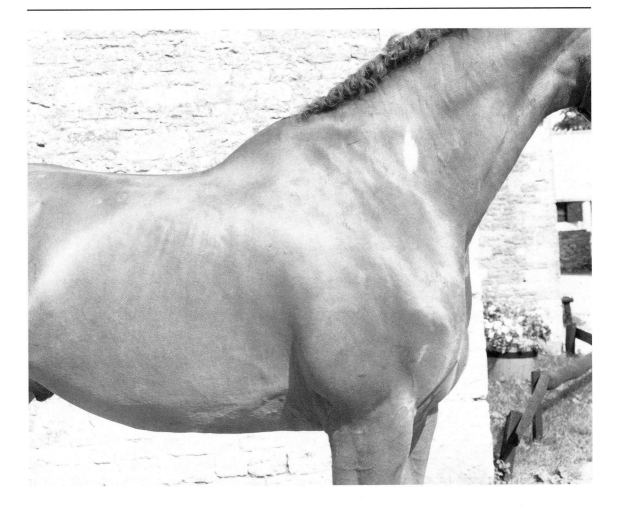

The shoulder

The shoulder must be strong, well muscled, and must lie at a good angle. The reasons for this are threefold:

1. A good, sloping shoulder will provide good suspension, whereas an upright shoulder will increase the effect of repeated concussion on the legs, knees, feet and tendons.
2. An upright shoulder gives a jolting ride, a sloping shoulder gives a smooth, well sprung ride.
3. A sloping shoulder of about 45° allows a free, elegant swing of the foreleg, so important in the competition horse. An upright shoulder inhibits this swing.

The barrel

In the competition horse it is vital that the barrel is full, round, well sprung and with a good heart-girth,

• **Fig 5** A strong, sloping shoulder – the wither is ideal for saddle fitting without being too prominent – and the barrel is well sprung

in other words, heart-room. It contains the animal's vital organs, and in particular the heart and lungs; any restriction in the function of either of these major organs will reduce the horse's physical efficiency. The breadth across the chest, between the forelegs, should be good but without being too wide – horses that are over-broad between the forelegs tend to have a rather rolling gait.

The rib-cage and its relevant muscles play an important part in breathing under pressure, and the ribs are therefore required to be well rounded. The horse that is described as 'slab-sided', where the ribs are flat and straight, is less likely to be able to use the rib-cage effectively in respiration.

Where the heart-girth is inadequate, the legs seem to be too long for the horse, and there appears to be too much daylight underneath him.

The neck should be neither too long and thin, nor too short and thick.

The wither should be well-defined, without being over-prominent.

The head should be of the correct size for that particular horse, neither too large nor too small. The shape of the head varies from breed to breed, but the general rules are relevant for all horses.

The shoulder must be well defined and lie at a good angle (about 45°).

● **Fig 6** The main points of conformation

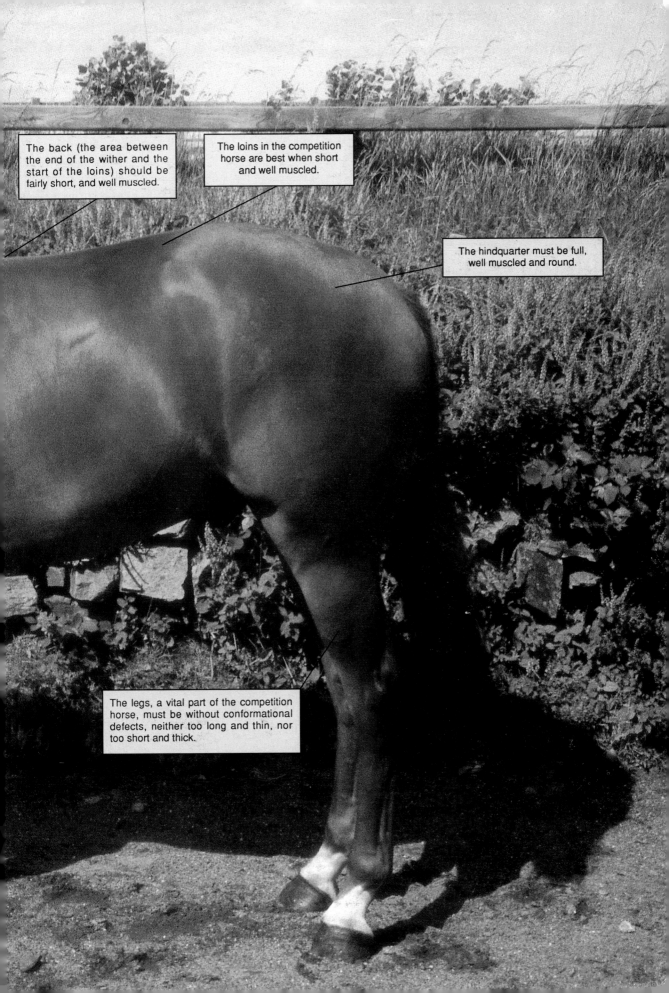

The back (the area between the end of the wither and the start of the loins) should be fairly short, and well muscled.

The loins in the competition horse are best when short and well muscled.

The hindquarter must be full, well muscled and round.

The legs, a vital part of the competition horse, must be without conformational defects, neither too long and thin, nor too short and thick.

The loins

Frequently when the horse's back is described as 'long', the real fault lies in the loins, and it is this area which is usually over-long and sometimes described as being 'slack'. Over-long loins are generally a weakness (unable to stand up to the rigours of competition training) and may prevent the horse from ever achieving really effective engagement of the hind legs.

The hindquarters

The hindquarters (including the croup, hips and tail) provide the main source of driving power. It is clear, therefore, that they should be big enough, well conformed and unblemished in the competition horse. In the Thoroughbred it is estimated that 16.6 per cent of his total body muscle is in the hindquarters and only 3.6 per cent in the shoulder.

The shape of the hindquarter varies between breeds: the Lipizzaner, for instance, has a rather square croup whilst the Thoroughbred has a more sloping croup. It is, in part, major differences in conformation such as this that suit the breeds to their individual tasks – the Thoroughbred to galloping, and the Lipizzaner to high collection and work above the ground, for example.

Some horses have a distinct bump at the point of the croup sometimes known as a 'goose rump' or a 'jumper's bump' – thought by some to be a sign of a good jumper. However, the point-of-croup should not be higher than the wither when the horse is 'standing up'. Nor should the horse have an overall tendency to slope naturally downhill: this is a disadvantage when trying to achieve good engagement of the hind legs.

The hips are the major joints through which the power created by the great muscles of the hindquarters is transmitted via the legs and feet to the ground. Even in the well covered horse the 'point of the hip' is prominent on each side and

● **Fig 7** There is a good length from hip to hock, the tail is well set on and the muscle development is excellent

prone to injury. Viewed from the rear, the points of the hips should be level: any deviation is a sign of injury, or is a conformational fault.

The tail often indicates the horse's mood and/or physical well-being. Also, it should be set on correctly for the specific breed: in some breeds it is set on higher, or lower, than in others – and in any case it should be set on straight and carried in a relaxed manner. A tail that is permanently twisted to the left or right, or carried unnaturally in some way, is usually an indication of tension, pain or conformational fault.

The back

In the competition horse this should be short, flat and well muscled, to provide the strength required to carry a rider and his saddle. The sprinter or the polo pony is usually a short-backed, close-coupled horse; the stayer is, as a rule, longer in the back. In fact a long back may give a more comfortable ride than a short back which may be found to give a rather jolting ride. In general the mare is longer in the back than the male horse, to facilitate the carrying of a foal.

Common faults found in the back are:

1 It is too long and weak. The excessively long back is a weakness because it will probably be more prone to injury and therefore less durable than a shorter back. It may prevent the horse from engaging the hind legs fully, thereby limiting impulsion and preventing him from achieving collection.

2 A 'roach' back: the spinal processes are obvious along the length of the back, and may cause problems with fitting the saddle. It is often associated with the 'slab-sided' horse, qv.

3 The 'hollow-' or 'sway-backed' horse is one in which the back shows a pronounced dip; it is a weakness and creates problems with saddle-fitting. It is often a feature of old horses.

The forelegs

Obviously, these limbs support the front end of the horse and play a part in locomotion at all paces: moreover at times, in canter and gallop and particularly when jumping, the entire weight of the horse, his rider and their equipment is supported, momentarily, on one foreleg. So when its appar-

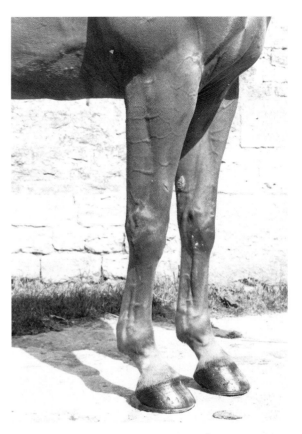

• **Fig 8** The forelegs are straight with good knees and 8½in of bone. The feet are an even pair with a good hoof/pastern axis

ently frail structure is considered, it may not seem so surprising that so much damage may be caused to the forelegs of the competition horse. Yet whilst the construction of the foreleg appears to be frail, it is in fact a masterpiece of engineering and is immensely strong. However, faults in its construction increase the effect of concussion upon it, rendering it more susceptible to strains of the suspensory elements (ligaments and tendons) and to degenerative joint disease.

Viewed from the front, each foreleg should be straight, ie a plumb-line dropped from the point of shoulder should fall straight down the front of the forearm, through the centre of the knee, down the centre of the cannon, fetlock joint, pastern, coronet and the centre of the hoof to the toe-clip of the shoe. Any deviation from this line caused by rotation or deviation of a joint may cause uneven wear on that joint and eventual disease and lameness. Minor faults of this nature may be corrected by corrective shoeing, qv.

The strong foreleg will have a long, well muscled forearm, a good knee and a short cannon with plenty of 'bone'. The measurement to assess 'bone' is taken round the cannon bone and back tendons immediately below the knee.

Faults in the conformation of the forelegs include bowlegs; knocked knees; pigeon-toes; toes turned out.

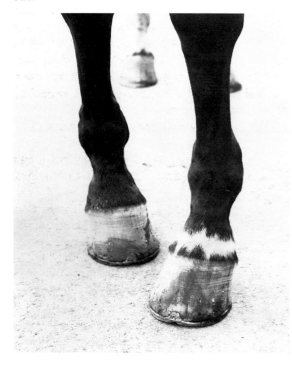

● **Fig 9** This picture shows very deformed lower legs. They are severely pigeon-toed with very worn fetlock joints

The knee: The conformation of the knee is important as it is a major, complex joint in the foreleg and subject to the strain of concussion at all paces and to external injury from impact when jumping. A good knee can be described as 'large, flat and near the ground': that is, it must be large enough for the horse that it has to carry; a 'flat' knee is usually a strong, unblemished joint; and if it is 'near the ground' it shows that the fore-arm is long and the cannon short.

Faults in the conformation of the knee include:

'*Over at the knee*', where the knee appears to be permanently flexed forward a little. Whilst some think this is unsightly, others consider it to be an advantage in the competition horse, since the forward tipping of the knee takes some of the strain off the back tendons. This conformation gives the impression that the horse may be caused to stumble, particularly when jumping. However, as long as the horse lands from a jump putting his heel down first, as he should, then stumbling is unlikely; it is the fault of putting the toe down first that causes the foreleg to buckle and the horse to stumble.

'*Back at the knee*': here, the knee appears to be permanently flexed a little to the rear of the tendons, and this is a serious condition for the competition horse because it causes excessive strain on the back tendons and extra pressure on the metacarpal bones at the front of the knee. It is a conformational fault that should be avoided in the selection of a potential competition horse.

'*Tied-in below the knee*': Summerhays' definition is the best: 'where the measurement immediately below the knee is less than the measurement taken lower down towards the fetlock joint'. This restriction below the knee may affect (adversely) the passage of the back tendons. The condition is often found in a horse that is light of bone, further compounding the fault.

The fetlock: The fetlock joints are also prone to concussion-induced wear, and any natural weaknesses present in these joints will make them less able to withstand such stress. They should be of a suitable size for a particular horse, and rounded rather than angular.

The pastern: should be long enough to provide good suspension, but not so long and sloping that it puts undue strain, by leverage, on the back tendons. On the other hand, short, upright pasterns give a jolting ride and are usually found with upright, boxy feet qv; this conformation of the pastern provides poor suspension and is prone to the adverse effects of concussion. The slope of the foreleg pastern should be parallel to the slope of the shoulder; this equates to about 50° in the forefoot – in the hind foot it should be about 55°.

The hind legs

Serious weakness in the hind legs will detract from the horse's ability to withstand the stress and strain of competition training. In general, the same rules apply to the hind legs as to the forelegs: first, in order to avoid excessive wear on the joints and eventual joint degeneration, the hind legs should be

• **Fig 10** A strong, well-muscled hindquarter. The competition horse must be well developed here as it is the source of his power

straight. A plumb-line dropped from the point of the buttock should pass down the hamstring, through the centre of the point of hock, down the centre of the cannon, through the ergot and should lastly bisect the heel. Sometimes the horse is 'cow-hocked' – that is, when viewed from behind the points of the hocks are turned inwards to meet one another; alternatively he may be 'bow-legged'. Both are bad faults tending to cause uneven joint wear.

Viewed from the side the horse may be seen to be 'sickle-hocked', ie the hock is curved instead of angular at the joint, rather like the blade of a sickle. Such a hock is generally found to be weak. Viewed from the side, a plumb-line dropped from the point of buttock should pass through the point of hock, and down through the ergot to the ground.

It is desirable for the horse to have good length from the point of the hip to the hock joint; this is sometimes described as being 'well let down'.

The gaskin, or second thigh should be well developed.

Any deformity of the hock joint is a severe disadvantage in a potential competition horse.

The feet

Good, strong, sound feet are very important in any horse, but they are vital in the competition horse since all four of his feet are put under considerable, unnatural strain whilst he is being prepared for, and taking part in, competition – they will be subject to strains of concussion, injury from sharp objects, injury from each other (brushing, over-reaching, speedy-cutting etc) and wrenching (perhaps in deep going).

The qualities of well conformed feet are that:

1 They are the correct size for the horse that they are required to carry, neither too small nor too big.
2 The hoof/pastern axis is good, ie the angle of the slope of the front of the hoof is a continuation of the slope of the pastern.
3 The horn growth is healthy.
4 There is a well developed frog.
5 The sole is concave (ie sloping up into the foot) never convex (tending to hang down).
6 They are an even pair; the fore feet being fairly round, the hind feet being more 'diamond'-shaped.
7 The toes point straight to the front, turning neither in nor out.

BLEMISHES

It is unlikely that a competition horse, in any discipline, will complete his career without eventually showing signs of wear or sustaining an injury scar. However, when selecting a potential competition horse there are some blemishes which it is well to avoid:

1 Fetlocks and hocks that show signs of wear, such as the various bursal enlargements; for example, windgalls and thoroughpins are usually an indication that the horse has been worked hard over a period of time.
2 Hocks that are spavined (this is not always superficially obvious). These are weak, and should be avoided.

LIBRARY
BISHOP BURTON COLLEGE
BEVERLEY HU17 8QG

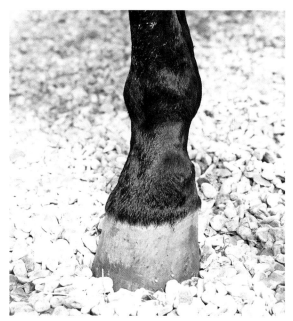

● **Fig 11** A severe ringbone, showing up here as a hard lump on the pastern. It is an incurable unsoundness

● **Fig 12** Proud flesh from an old injury just above the coronet on the off hind

3 Curby hocks are also a weakness and should be avoided.

4 Capped hocks and elbows are unsightly but will probably not detract from the horse's physical ability.

5 Bowed tendons (sometimes described as 'having a leg') are a sign of serious injury and should be avoided.

6 Signs of 'pin firing' or 'bar firing' are seldom now seen, but they are signs of drastic treatment to injured tendons. Horses showing these signs should be avoided as potential competition horses.

7 'Chipped knees' may be a sign of a habitual stumbler. This is clearly a sign of a horse to be avoided.

8 White saddle or bridle marks usually indicate careless management in the past, and should not impair the horse's ability other than in cases of serious injuries to the wither.

9 Scar tissue formed as the result of an old injury is unsightly, but should not impair the horse's ability to work – other than where it is so substantial that it restricts the use of a joint or the passage of the tendons.

10 'Splints' are usually the result of a trainer working his horse as a youngster too hard, and carelessly. Splints cause lameness when

they are forming but with professional care can usually be healed, and may even disappear. They can be a serious problem when they grow round the back of the cannon bone where they may interfere with the tendons.

● **Fig 13** A small splint on the inside of the near fore

STABLE MANAGEMENT

The competition horse in training will probably work for a minimum of two, to a maximum of three hours a day – 12½ per cent of the day. This means that 87½ per cent of the day he spends in his stable or the field, and the care that is taken of him during this 87½ per cent of his day dictates entirely what he can be asked to do during the 12½ per cent that he is worked. It is at least as important as his physical training and in some instances, more important.

STABLING FOR THE COMPETITION HORSE

It is possible, up to a certain level, to train a competition horse whilst keeping him out at grass. Indeed, many enthusiastic riders do this because their life-style limits the amount of time that they can spend on and with their horses. However, if he is to be trained for really serious competition work and the aim is to achieve the best possible performance that he can produce, he must be kept in a controlled environment, if only to regulate the amount and type of food that he consumes. It is difficult, if not impossible to work a horse sufficiently to maintain high muscle tone, combined with grooming and strapping, if he is out at grass full time and in all weathers. Most competition horses benefit from being turned out to grass regularly for two or three hours each day, to give them a period of natural relaxation; but the horse in serious training must essentially be stabled.

He requires a suitable loose box with good drainage and ventilation – that is, plenty of fresh air but no draughts. It should be well lit so he can be worked on when the days are short, or if he returns home from competition late at night. The internal fittings should be sufficient but not excessive, and must include a safe strip-light, 40 watt minimum; a feed manger and water manger, well secured but removable for cleaning purposes; and two tie-rings at about 1.6m above floor-level, fairly close together, one for a hay-net and the other for tying the horse up.

Stable doors should be not less than 2.25m (7ft) high and a minimum of 1.2m (4ft) wide, preferably 1.5m (5ft). The whole door is divided horizontally into two parts so that the top door can be left open; the bottom part should be not less than 1.2m high. Both doors should be fitted with bolts, the bottom door with two bolts, the lower one being a 'kick-bolt' which, for ease of use, is operated by the foot. The doors should open outwards and be fitted with hooks to secure them when they are open.

The minimum size for a loose-box for a 16hh middleweight hunter type is 3.75m (12½ft) square, and preferably 4m (13ft) square.

STABLE ROUTINE

Horses are creatures of habit and they do best if they are kept to a regular programme of exercise and feeding. Individual stable routines are designed to suit the needs of a particular yard and inevitably vary from yard to yard, but there are certain tasks that must be included daily in a stable programme. Here is a typical routine for a competition yard:

0700: Water and feed. Muck out. Quarter.

0845: Tack up ready for work.

0900–1100: Daily work exercise.

1130: Hay-nets and grooming.

1200: Skip out and midday feed.

1300: Turned out to grass, weather permitting, in New Zealand rugs if necessary. Or quiet in stables from 1400 to 1600.
Staff lunch.

1500: Bring in from grass. Hay-nets. Tack cleaning and other stable duties.

1700: Skip out. Afternoon feed.

2100: Skip out. Late night feed. Put in full hay-nets.

FEEDING THE COMPETITION HORSE

Competition horses make great demands on their diet. To cope with the stresses of training, travelling, competing and maintaining fitness over the competition season they need a higher-than-average intake of energy-giving food, of vitamins, minerals, amino acids and trace elements in a palatable and easily digestible form.

The technicalities of equine nutrition have, in recent years, been closely studied and much has been written of a technical nature in an attempt to maximise the advantages that the horse can derive from his feed. Yet in spite of all this detailed study, the most effective measure of whether or not the horse is doing well is still the eye of the experienced trainer.

The successful trainer will be aware of the answers to a number of basic questions relative to the feeding of the horse:

What is food expected to do for the horse?

Food must provide the energy that the horse needs to carry out his normal body functions – breathing, digesting, circulating blood etc – and to carry out the physical tasks that his trainer requires him to do.

It must provide replacement body tissue for that which is broken down every day in the rigours of competition training, and when necessary for repairing damage (healing).

Food must keep the horse warm. It is estimated that, in certain circumstances, up to 30 per cent of the food intake may go towards maintaining the body temperature.

The essential ingredients of the diet

Protein: This is the most important major component of the horse's diet. Protein consists of chains of smaller units known as amino acids, and the dietary requirement is for certain amino acids that cannot be produced by the body, lysine and methionine being the most important of these. Proteins are not all the same, and when considering protein in the diet it is important to take quality and digestibility into account as well as quantity.

The function of protein is to build new body tissue in growing horses; to replace worn-out body tissue in working horses; and to repair damaged tissue (healing injuries).

Most traditional horse feeds – eg oats, barley, hay etc – contain adequate protein for horses on a maintenance diet or light work. Horses in light work require about 8.5 per cent protein in the diet; pregnant mares about 10 per cent in the last 90 days of pregnancy, and 12 per cent at peak lactation; foals up to three months 16 per cent; and young maturing stock 10–12 per cent. Competition horses require a slightly higher-than-normal protein content to cope with the extra wear and tear of training, perhaps 10–12 per cent.

Energy-giving foods: These are provided in the form of carbohydrates which include starches, oils, fats and sugars. Their inclusion in the diet provides energy and warmth. The competition horse requires a high energy diet to enable him to gallop and jump and to provide the energy for training.

Minerals: Minerals and trace elements are essential, and are present to some degree in the normal diet. They include salt, calcium, potash, iron, zinc, sulphur, manganese, potassium, sodium, magnesium, iodine etc, all of which are required in the diet. In some areas of the country there may be a natural deficiency in one or more of these elements, though any absence can only be established by a veterinary blood test. As a deficiency of one of these may cause some form of debility in the horse (a shortage of iron, for example, may reduce the red cell blood count), it is as well for a blood test to be made from time to time. To feed one or more patent additives regularly without veterinary advice may prove expensive and counter-productive.

Vitamins: These are essential for the growth, development and health of all horses. They are required in small amounts only, but as each fulfils a different function they are all required. Vitamins occur in the natural diet but where a deficiency exists it can be rectified by feeding a supplement. This should only be done on veterinary advice, as to over-vitamin the horse may lead to unwelcome complications.

Water: The importance of feeding is well known and much time, effort and enterprise is put in to the production of horse feed. The importance of water in the diet is not so widely appreciated.

It has been recorded that a horse may survive for 30 days without food, but is unlikely to survive longer than 7 days without water. The average daily requirement for the stabled horse is between 10 and 14 gallons per day (4 to 5 stable buckets).

Water is a vital commodity in the diet for a number of reasons. The mature horse's body comprises between 65 and 75 per cent water. However, fluid is lost constantly from the body through staling, defecation, respiration and sweating (the larger the horse the greater the surface area from which sweat can evaporate), and this fluid loss must be replaced on a regular basis.

Throughout the digestive tract food must be in a very moist to liquid state for efficient digestion to take place. Saliva in the mouth plays a part in the early digestive stages, followed by digestive juices which are found in the stomach and small intestine, which produce the nutritious elements that can be absorbed into the body. Efficient digestion is impossible without sufficient water. Added to this, a shortage of water may cause colic and general dehydration resulting in debility and loss of condition.

All other vital body functions – respiration, blood circulation, the production of energy, muscle function, growth and repair of body tissues – all these depend on a regular supply of water.

• **Fig 14** The cross-country horse in 'tip-top' condition

The most desirable method of supplying water is to make it constantly available to the horse, either in buckets, a trough or via an automatic watering system. Whichever method is used, the container should be kept thoroughly clean and free from scraps of food, bedding or stale saliva. Individual watering is to be preferred to communal watering (a trough in the yard), to reduce the risk of cross-infection. Water should be fresh, clean and well aerated; it appears to matter little whether it is hard or soft, but horses usually do better in limestone areas in which the water is invariably hard. Cold water is usually preferred by horses, although some trainers like to take the chill off water that is being given to horses that come in, still warm, after hard work on a cold day.

To assist efficient digestion it is best that the horse should drink before feeding. The entrance to the stomach lies directly opposite the exit, the latter being larger than the former. If water is taken after feeding there is the possibility that undigested, or partially digested food will be washed through the stomach, which is wasteful. Furthermore, excessive water in the stomach dilutes the important digestive juices produced there, so reducing their efficiency.

The stomach lies high up the horse's body, separated from the lungs by the diaphragm. Should the horse be exercised whilst the stomach is full of water and/or food, pressure may be put on the lungs through the diaphragm, potentially causing irreparable damage to the lungs. A clear rest time of 1–2 hours should therefore be given between watering and feeding and strenuous exercise.

The amount of food required by the competition horse

The answer to this question depends entirely on the horse. There are, however, basic guidelines on which to base a calculation, and the most accurate guide to calculating the daily requirement in lb/kg is to consider the horse's bodyweight: the average horse requires 2.5 per cent of his bodyweight, in food, daily.

The most accurate way to assess the bodyweight is to take him in a truck or trailer to a weighbridge. Where this is not possible, two other adequate guides are available:

By measuring the girth: The bodyweight is relative to the girth measurement, which is taken just behind the wither and where the girth lies, but completely around the horse. The horse should be relaxed and the measurement taken as he exhales.

Girth		Estimated Bodyweight	
inches	cms	lb	kg
68	173	950	431
69	175	1000	454
70.75	180	1050	476
72	183	1100	499
73.25	186	1150	522
74.5	189	1200	544
75.75	192	1250	567
77	196	1300	590

By the use of the formula:

$$\frac{\text{Girth}^2 \times \text{length}}{300} = \text{bodyweight in lbs}$$

The length is the distance from the point of the shoulder to the point of the buttock in inches.

The total daily ration is then divided into two elements, 'concentrates' being the nutritious part of the feed, and 'roughage' the vital bulk part that makes efficient digestion possible and transports the nutritious elements through the digestive system.

Type of horse and work required	Roughage %	Concen-trate %
On a maintenance diet	60–80	40–20
Light work, hacking out 1–2 hours per day	50–60	50–40
Riding school horse, steady but not fast work	50	50
Competition horse in first month of training, up from grass and in soft condition	75 decreasing to 50	25 increasing to 50
In second month of training, getting fitter, working harder	50–40	50–60
Final month of training, fast work, galloping and jumping	40–30	60–70
Retention period, competition season, travelling and competing	40 or less	60 or more

The concentrates-to-roughage ratio varies widely, depending on the work that the horse is required to do; his temperament; the stage of his training.

The table on p24 is a broad guide, though it must be emphasised that the figures are intended as a guide only, and that they must be used in combination with experience, common sense and continual observation of the animal's condition and performance.

The types of food that may be included in the horse's daily ration

The horse in its natural state will live entirely on grass, and this will be sufficient to provide him with a balanced diet supplying all the essential ingredients to keep him healthy, strong, mobile and able to breed.

The ridden horse is taken into an unnatural environment and made to do physical work for which he was not designed, and so requires additional carbohydrate for energy and protein for repair. These have traditionally been provided in the form of oats, barley, maize, some other cereals, bran and hay. This type of diet has proved successful for many years, but it does have disadvantages:

1 These ingredients require individual weighing/ measuring and preparation.
2 It is difficult to assess their nutritional properties accurately.
3 It is not always possible to maintain a constant supply of each of the ingredients at a steady high quality over a long period of time.

The traditional diet has, to a large extent, been replaced by compounded cubes and mixes (pellets and sweet feeds). Produced in a wide variety of compounded ingredients, they cover the whole equine range from ponies to brood mares, youngstock, competition horses and racehorses. Each mix is designed with a particular task in view. They are popular and widely used for the following reasons:

1 Each diet is made for a particular purpose and contains a balance of energy, protein, vitamins, minerals and trace elements. They are balanced by the manufacturer, an impossible task for the average stable manager/trainer.

2 They are both extremely palatable and easily digestible.
3 As they are manufactured in large quantities the raw materials can also be purchased in large quantities, giving the manufacturer the opportunity to buy over a large area from various sources and consequently maintain continual high quality.
4 It is easy to measure out each feed, no mixing being required.

The disadvantages are that they tend to be more expensive than traditional feed, and that the shelf life, particularly of an open bag, is limited.

EFFICIENT FEEDING

The ten basic principles of efficient feeding are taught to every Pony Club member, and they are desirable for the well-being of all ponies and riding horses. For the competition horse these principles are vital and essential. They are reiterated here to underline their importance:

1 Divide the day's ration into several small feeds, no fewer than four. The horse's stomach is small, relative to his size, and his digestive system is designed to consume large quantities of cellulose and to digest it slowly over a longish period. In his natural state he grazes over most of the day, unlike the canines or felines who, in the wild, kill and eat once a day.
2 Provide a continuous supply of fresh, clean water. Between 65 and 75 per cent of the adult horse's body is water, and much is lost in sweat and evaporation during a day's work.
3 Feed only good quality food. Poor quality cereals and hay may contain impurities, dust or spores which are detrimental to the digestive and/or respiratory system. The nutritional value of poor quality food is invariably low, which is financially wasteful.
4 Be ready to provide for variety in the diet. Some horses are good doers and will eat a continuous ration enthusiastically; others are fussy feeders and need to be tempted – this is often so with the competition horse, as the strains of training are stressful and cause him to go off his feed. Some variety in the diet may help to keep it attractive to him.

LIBRARY
BISHOP BURTON COLLEGE
BEVERLEY HU17 8QG

5 | Changes in the diet should be made gradually to avoid upsetting the digestive system. The gut flora plays an important role in digestion and needs to adjust to suit a particular diet; this adjustment cannot be made immediately, since it requires a week to ten days to adapt itself.

6 | The ration should be kept palatable by the addition of a succulent element in each feed: sliced carrot, molasses, green food, linseed, raw egg or Guinness are succulents that may be considered.

7 | Each horse must be fed as an individual, taking into consideration his age, size, temperament, the amount and type of work that he is required to do, and the type of food that he finds palatable.

8 | Ensure that sufficient time is given for the horse to eat and digest his food before working him. A minimum of 1½ hours should be allowed after feeding before a competition horse is worked. It is best if only small feeds are given in the morning before ridden training begins, particularly if galloping or jumping are to be included in the work. The largest feed of the day should be the last feed at night, perhaps at 9pm, to allow all night for digestion.

9 | All feed rooms, cooking utensils, mangers, water troughs, feed scoops and other equipment used in feeding must be kept thoroughly clean to reduce the risk of contamination or infection.

10 | Horses are creatures of habit and do best if they are fed on a constant programme, the same number of feeds given at regular times each day.

These elementary rules play an important role in the feeding of the competition horse. Efficient feeding is an essential part of his training, and they are ignored at the trainer's peril.

SHOEING THE COMPETITION HORSE

Horses are shod for three basic reasons: to protect the foot; to improve the grip; and for surgical or corrective reasons.

To protect the foot

In his natural state, roaming freely over grassy plains, the horse's foot grows at a natural rate, the horn growing completely from the coronet to the bottom of the foot in about nine months. As he moves about grazing and exercising himself, the daily wear on the foot keeps it trimmed and healthy naturally. However, in circumstances where the horse is kept confined so that the foot is not worn down by exercise, the horn grows long and in extreme cases curls up at the toe. On the other hand, in the horse that is subjected to vigorous work, like the competition horse, the wear on the horn of the foot is certain to be greater than that which can be replaced by natural growth. Without shoes this would, other than in exceptional circumstances, result in the horse becoming footsore and eventually lame. The nailing of a band of iron (a horse shoe) onto the insensitive horn of the hoof has, for centuries, proved to be the most satisfactory means of protecting the foot from the unnatural wear put upon it by domestication and work.

The average competition horse will need to be shod about every four to six weeks, depending on a number of factors:

1 | The amount of work done on hard surfaces, such as a tarmac road, which accelerates wear of the shoes.

2 | The rate at which the horn grows; some horses grow horn at a faster rate than others. Even if the shoe is not worn out, it will need to be 'removed' – that is, taken off at four to six weeks so that the foot can be trimmed back to a good shape, and the old shoe then replaced. This is essential to ensure that the foot remains in balance qv.

3 | Uneven wear. Due to conformational faults or faulty action, some horses put uneven wear on the shoes which may make them unbalanced, even unsafe, and necessitates frequent re-shoeing to correct and maintain the balance.

4 | Feet that are shod with pads need more frequent attention than others.

To improve the grip

Like the runner on the track, or the footballer on the field, the competition horse requires a good grip for his foot on the ground. The natural design of the lower aspect of the foot provides adequate grip under natural circumstances, but the demands of competition riding necessitate a surer grip, particularly in fast work on slippery ground.

The competition horse is usually fitted with a hunter shoe. This is a shoe made from average-weight, fullered iron nailed on with seven nails. The number of nails may be altered in specific shoeing, but the general rule is that there should be as few as possible, but with enough to keep the shoe securely on the foot. The two extra sharp edges provided by the fullering increase the grip on the ground; also, the groove enables the nails to be driven well home. In the fullered shoe, two sides of the nail head are left exposed (unlike the stamped shoe), as this increases the grip on the ground.

Studs: The heels of both the fore and hind shoes may be drilled and tapped for studs. Studs are manufactured in a number of designs to suit particular conditions (see Fig 15). The rules for their use are as follows:

1 | When studs are worn they should be fitted to the shoe immediately before they are required to be used, and removed immediately afterwards. On hard going they unbalance the foot, and the horse is clearly in danger should he strike into himself with them. Under no circumstances should he be travelled wearing studs, as they would damage the floor of the horse-box. Small road studs may be permanently fitted to the heels of the shoe, as they are round and blunt making them unlikely to cause injury. They may, however, cause capped elbows when the horse lies down.

2 | Two studs should always be fitted to each shoe, one in each heel. The practice of fitting one stud to each foot in the outside heel may reduce the risk of injury from a stud fitted to the inside heel, but it causes serious lateral imbalance of the foot. The knee, fetlock and joints within the foot have little or no lateral flexion.

3 | The type of stud used should be as small as possible to achieve the required degree of grip.

4 | Stud holes should be plugged with cotton-wool or hemp when not in use, to prevent them becoming clogged with mud.

The use of the wedge heel and calkin is a good way of improving grip, provided that the balance of the foot is not spoilt by the over-raising of the heel.

● **Fig 15** A stud fitted to the outside heel of a hind shoe

The surgical or corrective reasons for shoeing

The well balanced foot is one where the natural hoof/pastern axis is maintained or enhanced. It is trimmed and shod in such a way that when the foot is on the ground the weight that it is required to carry is distributed evenly over its entire load-bearing surface.

Many types of specialist shoe have been designed as a result of consultation between the veterinary surgeon and the farrier in an attempt to relieve problems in the feet and to improve the foot balance. The most common that may be encountered by the trainer of competition horses are as follows:

1 *The seated-out shoe* and the *threequarter shoe.* These are made to relieve pressure on the seat of corn.
2 *The cross-bar shoe* gives added sole support to wide flat feet.
3 *The rolled-toe shoe* helps the lazy horse that tends to drag his toes and stumble.
4 *The feather-edged shoe* reduces the danger of injury caused by brushing.
5 *The diamond-toe* hind shoe helps the horse that 'forges' ie strikes into the inside of the toe of the fore shoe with the toe of the hind shoe.
6 *The 'T' shoe* puts pressure on the frog, helping with circulation in the relief of contracted heels.
7 *The speedy-cutting shoe*: some horses through faulty action when galloping strike into the upper cannon or lower knee with the inside quarter of the opposite shoe (usually on the fore legs only): this is known as 'speedy-cutting'. This special shoe has the inner branch, where the toe and quarter join, made straight, removing the iron which causes the injury. This branch is usually blind, that is without nails, though there may be one or two nails at the heels.
8 *Close-fitting shoes*: 'Close-fitting' is when the shoe is set slightly under the wall of the foot. It is most often used on the inner branches when the horse is inclined to brush – it is a useful precaution to fit the inner branches of the hind shoes closer rather than wider in all competition horses.

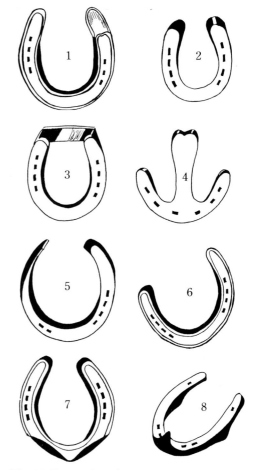

• **Fig 16 Corrective shoes**
1 The 'eased shoe'. This is designed to relieve the pressure from the seat of corn.
2 The shoe for navicular disease. This is thick at the heels and thinner at the toe, transferring more of the horse's weight to the front of the foot.
3 The 'pattern shoe'. This shoe raises the heels and takes the strain off the back tendons. The horse cannot be worked in this shoe. It can only be fitted when he is at rest.
4 The 'T' shoe. This puts pressure on the frog and helps to relieve contracted heels. It also takes the weight off both seats of corn.
5 The 'feather-edged' shoe. The inside heel of this shoe is taken away to reduce the possibility of injury being caused by a horse that brushes.
6 The 'three-quarter' shoe is fitted to take the pressure off the seat of corn or to prevent injury from brushing.
7 The 'diamond toe' shoe. This is a hind shoe on which the toes have been recessed to relieve the effects of 'forgeing', that is when the toe of the hind shoe strikes into the inside of the toe of the fore shoe, particularly when trotting.
8 The 'rocker' shoe. This shoe is fitted when it is necessary to keep the joints in the foot and the fetlock mobile. Its rocking effect keeps the joints moving. It is used in cases of ankylosis, ringbone, laminitis etc.

The use of hoof pads: There are a number of circumstances in which it is necessary to protect the bearing surface of the competition horse's feet. For example, some horses have thin or dropped soles which bruise easily, and these can be protected by fitting a thin pad of leather or plastic between the foot and the shoe. This pad protects the sole and/or the frog and provides some general relief from the effects of concussion when working on hard or stony ground.

The disadvantages of fitting pads are that they make the nailing on of the shoe less secure; and the maintenance of foot hygiene is made difficult, as the foot is deprived of air and cannot be regularly picked out.

There is no doubt that training a horse to competition fitness subjects his respiratory, circulatory and digestive systems to unnatural strain. And no matter how knowledgeable and careful the trainer is, competition training will definitely put unnatural wear and tear on the horse's feet. Careful care of the feet and expert shoeing can reduce the effects of this strain, helping the horse to perform better and last longer. It is even possible in some cases, by close co-operation between the veterinary surgeon and the farrier, to correct faults in the conformation of the foot that are either natural or the result of poor husbandry. By gradually raising or lowering the heels or toes, the hoof/pastern axis may be improved. Lateral adjustments of the foot may also be made by varying the thickness of the branches of the shoe. To avoid uneven wear of the joints it is important that a line drawn horizontally through the coronary band should be parallel to the ground. Where this is not so, careful shoeing may help to correct it. However, both the veterinary and farriery professions are of the opinion that to make this type of adjustment requires the treatment to be carried out during three complete growths of horn. As has already been said, it takes nine months for the horn to grow completely from the coronet to the ground; which means that a satisfactory result is unlikely to be achieved in less than two years and three months.

To remain sound the horse's feet must be well balanced, ie they must be trimmed and shod in such a way that when supporting the weight of the horse the load is distributed evenly over the entire bearing surface of each foot.

VETERINARY CARE OF THE COMPETITION HORSE

Equine veterinary science is a wide, complicated subject and it is inadvisable for the trainer or rider to attempt to be his own veterinary surgeon. Nevertheless, an elementary knowledge of the horse's anatomy and physiology, and an appreciation of the strains put upon it under competition training conditions, help the trainer to recognise when something is wrong, or better still, about to go wrong. And to be able to recognise when the condition is abnormal, he must first be able to recognise the normal signs of health in the horse. These might be itemised as follows:

1 The horse should be bright and alert, paying attention to what is going on around him without being nervous. If he is dull and standing in the corner of his box with his ears back, head down and tail clamped down, all is *not* well.

2 The eyes should be bright, clear and free from discharge.

3 The nostrils should be clean and free from discharge.

4 The mucous membrane around the eye, nostrils and the inside of the lips should be salmon pink in colour. If it is red, suspect inflammation; if it is pale, suspect a low red blood cell count.

5 The skin should be soft and move freely over the underlying tissues, and the coat should be soft and shiny.

6 His stance should be normal. One hind leg is often rested, but very seldom a foreleg unless it is in pain.

7 Dung should be passed about eight to ten times a day. It should be neither too hard nor too loose – as a guide, the droppings should break as they hit the ground.

8 Urine should be passed without strain or difficulty; it should be straw-coloured, and free from strong smell.

9 Temperature, pulse and respiration rates should remain normal.

10 There should be no drastic change in the appetite for either food or water.

11 Sudden changes in temperament are usually a sign that all is not well, and any change from normal should be watched carefully.

The main areas in which domestication and competition training may affect the horse's health are his digestive system, his respiratory system and the system of support and locomotion.

The digestive system

The horse's system is designed to take in large quantities of cellulose which it then proceeds to process slowly over a period of time. However, to ensure that the domesticated horse is provided with sufficient nutrition, he is fed an unnatural diet, and one of the risks is that this frequently causes a condition known as 'colic' which is both painful and dangerous. It is not a specific disease, but a condition occurring somewhere in the alimentary tract caused by a blockage of food or gas which as it builds up in pressure, causes pain. It may be just a mild 'stomach ache', or it may be a serious impaction requiring urgent veterinary attention; but all cases should be treated as serious. Possible symptoms are lying down and rolling excessively; biting at the flank and kicking at the belly; breaking out in patchy sweat; and probably the pulse rate will rise.

The first-aid treatment is to try to relieve the pain, and this may be achieved by leading out in hand. If this is not successful and the symptoms are not relieved in half an hour, or if the pulse rate rises to 50 beats per minute, then veterinary help should be sought.

Horses that are prone to recurrent colic require careful feeding and constant monitoring.

The respiratory system

Whilst the horse was designed to gallop, he was not designed to gallop over long distances carrying a heavy load. But this is, in fact, what competition work requires of him, and his respiratory system in particular is put under unnatural strain when training and competing. So a sound respiratory system is a fundamental requirement of the competition horse, and it is therefore important to protect him from the threat of infection, physical strain, and also from dust and lack of fresh air which may impede his ability to breathe efficiently.

Infection is either viral or bacterial. Viral infections include influenza and equine herpes; bacterial infections include strangles, pneumonia and the common cold. Bacterial infections frequently follow viral infections, but whereas bacterial infections can be treated with antibiotics, viral infections cannot.

Equine influenza: This is a serious condition which occurs from time-to-time as an epidemic. It is highly contagious and spreads rapidly. Animals which are not inoculated against equine influenza are barred from entry to race-courses and other equestrian premises. The symptoms of this disease are a deep cough, discharge from the nostrils, high temperature, loss of appetite and deep depression. Veterinary help must be sought, the animal should be isolated and normal sick-nursing duties carried out. Recovery is often protracted and the horse may, in some cases, not be back in full work for three months.

Chronic obstructive pulmonary disease (COPD) (heaves): An unhindered supply of oxygen is required by any horse, but particularly by the competition horse to enable him to burn up the sugars stored in the muscles and so create energy. This supply of oxygen is sometimes partially blocked by certain conditions in the airways ie the bronchi, bronchioles and alveoli. These blockages may be caused by mucus in the airways, or by tightening or inflammation of the airways.

The inside of the airways is normally lined with a watery fluid known as mucus, which traps dust and bacteria and transports them out of the body via the throat. When the horse is suffering from a respiratory condition this mucus becomes thick, sticky and is slow to move; it blocks the tubes to the lung, restricts the flow of oxygen and causes the horse to cough. It can be liquefied by drugs known as 'mucolytics'.

The tubes of the airways are made of muscle. When diseased, the muscles become very sensitive and contract, blocking the passage of oxygen and causing the horse to wheeze. This condition is referred to as *bronchospasm*. Drugs known as 'bronchodilators' are available to relieve this condition.

When infected, the airways may become red, sore and swollen, again restricting the passage of air. This can be eased by the use of anti-inflammatory drugs.

A horse suffering from the conditions described above will probably betray one or more of the following symptoms:

1 Distressed breathing. The breathing of the healthy horse at rest is hardly visible, and there should be no flaring of the nostrils. The fit horse, at rest, breathes about 8–14 times per minute.

2 Wheezing is a common sign of respiratory disease and is associated with stabled horses in dusty conditions.

3 Coughing. Fit horses rarely cough; even an occasional, slight cough is a sign that something is wrong.

4 Nasal discharge. Thick, discoloured discharge is a sign of infection.

5 The heaves line. This is a deformity of the line of muscle running roughly from the point of the elbow back along the lower edge of rib-cage towards the stifle. It is caused by the horse using that muscle group excessively to help with impaired breathing.

Early recognition of a respiratory condition is vital, and veterinary help should be sought. There are a number of precautions that can be taken to reduce the risk of respiratory conditions occurring:

1 Maintain a dust-free stable environment. Avoid straw bedding: straw contains millions of spores to which some horses are allergic. Wood shavings, paper or peat are all acceptable bedding alternatives.

2 Damp all feeds and soak all hay.

3 Keep horses that are prone to these conditions out at grass as much as possible.

4 Avoid work in dusty schools or arenas, and give your horse a weekly 'pipe opener' where appropriate.

A condition known as 'broken wind' affects some horses, and is normally caused by galloping young or unfit horses excessively. This results in the break-down of the alveoli which line the lungs and through which gasses are exchanged. The condition is irreversible, and the sufferer would not be capable of being trained as a competition horse.

Lameness

Perhaps the parts of the horse's anatomy that are most susceptible to damage when he is trained for competition are the legs and feet, the limbs that support and propel him. The bones, joints, tendons and ligaments that make up these limbs are subject to the effects of concussion by repeated pounding, wrenching and twisting, and percussion by hitting jumps, or falling.

Lameness is nearly always due to pain, and it is essential that the trainer/rider is able to identify the presence of pain by noticing an alteration in the horse's gait. Pain will cause the horse to try to relieve the weight that the affected limb has to bear: this results in him lifting his head as a lame foreleg comes to the ground, or lifting a hip as a lame hind leg comes to the ground. This is best detected when the horse is trotting, as only two legs are supporting his bodyweight at any one time at this pace. When he is walking he will have three feet on the ground at any one time, thus spreading the bodyweight more evenly. However, severe lameness will show at walk.

When the lame leg has been identified, the seat of lameness can often be diagnosed by the presence of heat, pain, and/or swelling. Heat can be felt by touch, comparing one limb with the other; swelling can be seen, and pain can be detected by careful palpation. Veterinary help should be sought in all but the most elementary situations that cause lameness.

Common causes of lameness include:

1 Pus in the foot: an infection inside the wall of the foot causing heat and pressure.

2 Corns and bruised soles; caused by concussion.

3 Arthritic conditions in the joints brought about by concussion; wear and tear over a long period; thrombosis; congenital weakness; poor conformation; and misuse. These conditions commonly include ringbone, navicular disease, pedal ostitis, sesamoiditis and bone spavins.

4 Sprains of joints, ligaments or tendons. Joints are usually sprained by twisting or wrenching. Ligaments and tendons are sprained by stretching them beyond their current limits of elasticity.

5 Damage to the foot, including poor shoeing (eg a nail bind or a pricked foot), advanced thrush, a foreign body in the foot (eg a stone lodged in the cleft of frog), a puncture wound in the foot, cracked or greasy heels, sand cracks, grass cracks, seedy toe, quittor or laminitis.

The treatment of lameness depends on the diagnosis, but may include the following: the elimination of infection; rest; electrical treatment; steroid therapy; graduated exercise; manipulation/ physiotherapy; cold laser treatment; Faradism; and surgery.

GROOMING AND STRAPPING

This is the daily care of the horse, and is essential for his physical well-being. It can be divided into three distinct sections: quartering; daily grooming; and strapping.

Quartering

Quartering comprises one of the first morning tasks; in a normal stable routine, at 7am the horse is watered, fed, mucked out and quartered. Quartering consists of picking out the feet and removing bedding from the mane and tail, and cleaning off night stains: without removing the stable-rugs completely, first undo the breast strap and fold the front half back, allowing the forequarter to be brushed with the body brush. The front half of the rug is replaced, then the fillet string is removed and the back half of the rug folded forward, and the hind quarter brushed with the body brush and the rug replaced. Night stains are then brushed off the legs. This is done for the sake of good order and general cleanliness.

Full grooming

Full grooming is done daily, usually after work as it will be more efficient if the horse has sweated and dried off. It then leaves him clean and fresh for the rest of the day. Full grooming, when done thoroughly by a competent groom, takes about 45 minutes. The objects of grooming are several: to promote health by keeping the horse clean, removing mud, sweat-residue and so on; to massage the skin and underlying muscle; and to promote local blood circulation, and the healthy growth of the coat. It also gives the groom a daily opportunity to inspect the horse all over in detail. It is a good training in obedience and stable manners, establishing trust between the horse and groom.

The skin is the single largest organ in the horse's body, and its healthy condition is a vital part of his well-being. In the healthy horse it should be soft and supple, and should move freely over the underlying tissues; the coat itself should shine. The skin fulfills a number of important tasks: it protects and plays a part in supporting the organs and tissues that make up the whole body; it helps to regulate the body temperature; its waterproof qualities retain the body fluids when required, and it provides a protective cover for the animal; the coat that it grows provides warmth; the skin – and particularly the hair – are sensitive organs of touch.

The thickness of the skin varies considerably over the horse's body, being up to 12mm thick over the back and loins where maximum protection is required, down to only 3mm over the face and lower legs. It consists broadly of two layers, the epidermis on the surface and the dermis immediately below. The epidermis is largely dead tissue which is being cast as scurf; its main purpose is to stop the passage of fluids through the skin. The dermis contains the sweat glands, nerves and blood vessels.

Sweat glands are distributed generously all over the horse's body. They are activated by adrenalin (secreted by the adrenal glands and circulated in the bloodstream) which allows the horse to sweat, cooling him and expelling other mineral substances from the body.

Sebaceous glands produce sebum, the substance that is secreted from the dermis thus keeping the skin waterproof and pliable, and the coat glossy.

The horse's hair varies in type from the thick hair of the mane, tail and feather, to the finer hair of the coat covering the body, and the sensitive hair of the whiskers on the muzzle. The hair of the mane, tail and body provides warmth and protection. The whiskers on the muzzle are very sensitive and help the animal to locate and identify its food, and the mare to nuzzle and recognise her foal. The hair of the mane and tail is permanent, but the body hair is shed regularly, depending on climatic conditions. Hair and skin vary in texture between breeds and types; for example the Arab and Thoroughbred tend to have fine skin and hair, whereas in the heavier breeds it is usually coarser.

An understanding of the vital functions of the skin and coat emphasises the importance of their condition, and hence the necessity for thorough daily grooming.

The feet: As well as care of the skin and coat, daily grooming must include regular care of the feet. These should be picked out several times a day, and once a week the sole and frog area should be scrubbed out and treated with an astringent antibiotic dressing to discourage thrush. The walls of the hoof should be brushed clean and treated with hoof oil to protect the periople and encourage healthy horn growth.

The eyes, nose, muzzle, and dock should be sponged at least once daily with separate sponges.

In the male horse, the sheath should be washed about once a quarter, more frequently if necessary. A strong-smelling black substance called smegma is secreted into the sheath which, when combined with dust and dirt, collects as a hard ball. This sometimes discourages the horse from 'letting down' to urinate, compounding the problem; it is unhygienic and may cause discomfort. Wash the inside of the sheath with medicated soap and a sponge to remove the offending hard ball, then rinse thoroughly with warm water.

Strapping

This is a form of massage, and can be used on the horse as part of his daily grooming once he is beginning to get fit and is developing his muscles. It stimulates local blood circulation in the skin, helps muscle development and brings a shine to the coat. It is used on major muscle areas only, ie on either side of the neck, on either side of, and below the wither, and on the major muscle groups of the croup and hind quarters. It should not be used on soft areas, or where the bones and joints are near the surface.

Strapping can be done with a hay wisp, a folded stable rubber or a special leather grooming or strapping pad. Hold the pad in one hand and bring it down with a solid bang on the muscle area, sliding it off the skin in the direction in which the coat lies. It should be introduced lightly and slowly, increasing the strength of the bang as the horse accepts it; put the whole bodyweight behind each stroke and work in a steady rhythm. This encourages the horse to tense his muscles in anticipation of the bang, and relax them again at the end of the stroke. In the initial stages, ten or twelve strokes will be sufficient in each area, increasing to twenty to twenty-five as the work progresses.

Washing horses

This is sometimes necessary and is often beneficial, particularly in hot weather when the horse has sweated. It is essential that facilities are available to get him dry afterwards. Where possible warm water should be used, as cold water closes the pores and discourages sweating. A hosepipe is an ideal way of applying the water but where the horse objects to this, buckets must be used. Soft medicated soap is ideal; any soap containing a detergent should be avoided. Several medicated horse shampoos are available. Once all the soap has been rinsed off, he should be dressed in a sweat rug and walked in hand until dry. Particular attention must be paid to drying the legs: note that if the horse returns from work with muddy feet and legs, washing with a hose-pipe may cause cracked heels and general chapping of the skin, unless facilities exist to dry the legs thoroughly. It is better to apply stable bandages over the mud, allow the legs to dry and brush the dry mud off later.

Whilst washing removes dirt and dust and leaves the horse fresh and clean, it is not a substitute for grooming.

THREE

GETTING THE COMPETITION HORSE FIT

Fitness for the competition horse is a very broad term covering a wide range of competition requirements. 'Fit for what?' is the first question to be answered, since the fitness requirement differs considerably between flat-race horses, steeplechasers, polo ponies, showjumpers, dressage horses, hunters, riding school horses, hacks, show ponies – and so the list goes on. Moreover in horse trials, showjumping and dressage the level of fitness required at novice level is very much less than that required at advanced level.

Nevertheless, there are certain basic principles common to most, even all, disciplines which will be considered here. Therefore in an attempt to cover these principles, a normal, uncomplicated horse will be considered in his training for horse trials at intermediate level. This will enable some consideration to be given to dressage, showjumping and cross-country training.

The novice event horse does not need to be particularly fit. If he is ridden seriously for about 1½ hours a day, 6 days a week and his work includes dressage training, jumping training and some cross-country work he will naturally become fit enough for a one day event. The timetable drawn up here should be considered as a broad rule of thumb, to be adjusted and amended intelligently, using one's knowledge and experience, to suit a particular set of circumstances. It starts with a completely unfit horse, takes him through a pro-

Conditioning	Hardening-up	Improving the Wind	First competition day etc	Retention of Condition
4–5 weeks. Walk and slow trot ¾–2hr.	4–5 weeks roadwork, 2 hours daily.	4–5 weeks. Long canter 12 minutes.		12 weeks. Keep fresh. Reduce road work. Lead out in hand. Pipe-openers. Hacking out.
Oats 2–4kg (4½–9lb) Bran 1–1.5kg (2–3½lb) Hay 4.5–5.5kg (10–11lb) Green food. Cubes Mixes. Limestone-flour, cod liver oil etc.	Slow canters. School work supplying and gymnastic exercises. Light cub-hunting.	Gallops up to 1¼ miles, slow ¾ mile, fast ¼ mile, slow down ¼ mile. Jump schooling.		Keep diet light, fresh and tempting.
Shoeing, clipping, teeth rasping. Influenza and tetanus moculations. Blood and urine tests	Interval training. Oats 4.5–7.25kg (10–16lb) Bran 1–1.5kg (2–3½lb) Hay 6.5kg (14½lb)	Decrease hay to 4.5kg (10lb). Generally decrease bulk and increase concentrates.		Turn out to grass for 2 hours per day.
Grooming and strapping.	Vitamins. Cubes. Mixes. Linseed etc.			

• **Fig 17** An excellent type of potential competition horse

gramme that includes his first competition day, and continues into the competition season. It would be a suitable broad outline plan for a novice horse.

The horse to be considered is an eight-year-old, 16hh bay gelding, by a Thoroughbred stallion out of a half-bred Irish Draught/Thoroughbred mare. He is of good temperament, and has no blemishes or conformational faults that might adversely affect his training. He was well handled as a foal, and was shown at foot with his dam. He was then shown in-hand as a two-year-old, backed at three years old, and turned away until four when serious ridden training began. At five years old he was lightly cub-hunted, he took part in some preliminary dressage and novice showjumping, and was hacked out regularly. At six years old he continued in novice dressage, showjumping and novice horse trials. At seven years old he competed successfully in horse

trials gaining 22 points, and is now a 'Grade 2' horse. He has been turned out to grass for three months.

The aim of training this horse is to get him ready for an Intermediate horse trial in three months' time. It is now 1 January and the first competition is on 1 April.

BRINGING THE HORSE UP FROM GRASS

Having been out at grass for three months he has been thoroughly 'let down' – that is, he is fat and soft. He will have a long coat and a good covering of sebum etc over his skin; he has been on a high fibre/low concentrate diet and is unshod. During his forthcoming training his environment, condition

35

and way of life will be changed completely, and it is important that these changes are made gradually and progressively.

His preparation starts whilst he is in the field. As it is January, he will be having a regular supply of good hay, but comparatively little in the way of concentrates. To ensure that his diet is changed gradually, he will therefore be fed some concentrate over the last two weeks he is still at grass. This may take the form of about 1kg (2.2lb) of 'Horse and Pony' cubes, or an oats/bran/chaff mix, or boiled barley if it is very cold. He may have to be brought in for his food if he is in a field with other horses that are not being fed.

In this two-week period it is as well to ensure that all is ready for when he comes in full-time. His loose box should be checked and prepared, bedding and forage ordered, rugs and tack and clippers checked. It is a good plan to have him looked over by the veterinary surgeon at an early stage, perhaps when he is given his anti-tetanus and equine influenza inoculation; if necessary his teeth can be rasped and a blood test made too.

To avoid frustrating delays in the training programme, the blacksmith should be booked well in advance; make this arrangement in these first preparatory two weeks so that the horse can be shod as soon as he is brought in.

To ensure that the change in his lifestyle is gradual, for the first week he will be brought in at night, fed and turned out during the day. If he has been wearing a New Zealand rug in the field this will be replaced by a stable rug at night. The stable top door will be left open, ensuring good ventilation but no draughts. The New Zealand rug will be replaced when he is turned out to grass during the day.

At the end of this week he can be brought in full time but will probably still be turned out to grass for two hours a day, maybe in the afternoon, weather permitting.

INITIAL ADMINISTRATION

The necessary administrative tasks can now be undertaken in order that the horse's serious training can start.

Feeding

The diet should be changed gradually from his grass diet to the higher concentrate diet that he will need as training progresses. The horse that is being considered probably weighs approximately 1,200lb (545kg); if he requires 2.5 per cent of his bodyweight in food daily, his daily ration will therefore be a total of 30lb (13.5kg). Over the first week to ten days his ration will be increased from a permanent haynet of good quality hay plus 2–3lb (1–1.5kg) of Horse and Pony nuts per day, to a 'maintenance' diet, thus ensuring that not too much concentrate is introduced too quickly. At about ten days the concentrate/fibre ratio should therefore be 50/50: that is, 15lb (6.75kg) concentrate, 15lb (6.75kg) fibre.

A specimen daily ration to be achieved by ten days might be:

07.30   3lb (1.4kg) Horse and Pony nuts (these contain approximately 15 per cent fibre)

10.00   After morning work, 5lb (2.5kg) haynet (good hay)

12.00   3lb (1.4kg) Horse and Pony nuts, 1lb (0.5kg) green food or carrots, 5lb haynet

16.00   3lb (1.4kg) Horse and Pony cubes, 1lb (0.5kg) green food or carrots

21.00   3lb (1.5kg) Horse and Pony cubes, 1lb (½kg) bruised oats, 1lb (0.5kg) sugarbeet pulp (soaked), 1 tablespoon cod liver oil, 5lb (2.5kg) haynet.

This diet is a guide only and *must* be tailored to suit the individual horse.

Veterinary Care

At this stage the horse should be checked over by the veterinary surgeon and given his anti-tetanus and equine influenza inoculation. This usually means that he is rested for 48 hours and then only walked out in hand for a further five days. In no circumstances should he be allowed to sweat during this period.

Teeth: The molar teeth are an important early stage in efficient digestion. A horse's teeth grow constantly, and can become sharp at the edges, possibly causing discomfort when chewing. This can lead to insufficient mastication of the food, and impair good digestion. It is a simple operation for the veterinary surgeon to rasp off the sharp edges on the molar teeth with a special rasp.

Blood and urine samples should be taken at this stage, and at regular intervals throughout the horse's training (on the veterinary surgeon's recommendation), for laboratory analysis. These tests will reveal certain levels of enzymes and electrolytes, knowledge of which is a major advantage in the horse's training. For example:

Enzymes are emitted into the bloodstream by the body tissues. They are proteins that are produced by the living cells to promote specific biochemical reactions in the body without undergoing change themselves ie they are catalysts. One particular muscle enzyme is creatine kinase (CK), which is emitted into the bloodstream when the muscle is damaged or put under strain. Thus the amount of CK emitted is in proportion to the degree of damage or strain, and by measuring the amount of CK in the blood the veterinary surgeon can derive information to assist in diagnosing muscle damage, and can also measure progress in physical fitness. As the horse gets fitter, less CK is emitted into the bloodstream for a given amount of work.

Electrolytes are natural body salts (that is, sodium, potassium, calcium etc) which are vital for correct functioning of the muscles. An electrolyte imbalance in the competition horse, brought about by sweating or stress, may result in loss of muscle efficiency or in damage. These deficiencies are best discovered by laboratory urine analysis, a precaution which has been particularly successful in preventing occurrences of azoturia/setfast/tying-up in horses that are prone to this condition.

Accurate blood and urine analysis enables the veterinary surgeon to recommend a particular feed additive that will help to relieve any chemical imbalance within the body. The ad lib/haphazard feeding of additives and vitamin supplements can be expensive, wasteful and counter-productive.

Shoeing

The horse's feet are trimmed, and he is shod with hunter shoes. The farrier will take note of any special requirements and will discuss future shoeing plans. If necessary, the veterinary surgeon and farrier will consult with one another and may agree a plan to help with long-term correction or improvement of the feet. It is generally accepted that corrective shoeing will not yield results in less than three complete growths of horn. As it takes nine months or thereabouts for the horn to grow from the coronet to the ground, progress should not be expected in less than 27 months.

Clipping

As it is now the end of January there are still eight weeks of winter weather to go. The horse must be clipped in order that work can start, but he must be left with sufficient coat cover to prevent him getting cold at night or when he is turned out during the day. The legs and head should be left as these are difficult to keep warm artificially. The most practical clip, at this stage, is a 'chaser clip where the gullet and front of the neck are clipped out, together with the chest, belly and between the hind legs, areas in which the horse may sweat. The object is to keep the horse warm, but to enable him to work without getting over-hot, which creates a problem in getting him dry after work.

Tack and Equipment

If care is not taken, fitting a bridle, saddle and boots to an unfit horse may cause rubbing and consequently sores that can delay ridden work. All leather tack must be soft and pliable. Remember that the saddle that fits the horse when he is lean and fit is probably unsuitable when he is fat and unfit. Also, particular care must be taken with the girth that is fitted to an unfit horse, as it will almost certainly need to be longer than the girth that he will use when he is fit; a girth that is too loose or too tight will almost certainly cause a girth gall on a fat, soft horse. Similarly if it is hard or dirty it will rub; fitting a sheepskin sleeve to the girth is often a sensible precaution. Leather, plastic or nylon boots may also rub and cause discomfort.

Diligent cleanliness, preparation and care will reduce these risks to the minimum.

Grooming

A routine of light grooming can be started, to clean off surface dirt and begin to remove the greasy layer from the skin, enabling the horse to sweat more easily. His work will not be hard enough to make him sweat copiously for some time yet, but grooming promotes health and improves his appearance. The mane and tail can be pulled and trimmed, and the feather (if any exists) can be removed. The washing of eyes, nose and dock and the male horse's sheath are always important for his well-being. Pick out the feet regularly.

STARTING WORK

Having completed the preparatory administration, the 12–15 week training and preparation programme will be divided into three pre-competition periods, as shown in the diagram on pp 39–41.

Conditioning (weeks 1–4)

It is often tempting, but *always* a mistake, to hurry this initial four to five week conditioning period. Even if the horse appears to want to go on and do more, the temptation must be resisted – there will be plenty of hard work for him to take on board in the next two months. A slow, methodical build-up of muscle and tendons *now*, will make a firm basis for the strenuous work to come.

Hardening-up including Interval training
(weeks 5–9)

At this stage it is often helpful to start on a programme of interval training, the broad principles of which are explained here.

Interval training was first used in the 1930s by Scandinavian athletes. It is intended to build up condition/fitness without subjecting the athlete to the strain of training over the competition distance at competition pace. The work consists of measured periods of work interspersed with measured periods of rest. The pulse rate is recorded at the start and finish of each period of work, and the rest period allows the pulse rate to return to, or towards, normal. As fitness improves the pulse returns to normal (or near normal) more quickly, and this enables the trainer to decide when, and how, the work-load can be increased. He can either: make the distance covered in the work period longer; make the work period faster; or reduce the time of the rest period.

Under training conditions, the horse's pulse rate is less easy to record than a human athlete's, and it is helpful if the trainer, or another assistant, is present to assist with this task. A stethoscope is an essential piece of equipment for listening to the heart. Alternatively a pulse meter is available which enables the pulse rate to be counted by a sensor in a pad attached to the girth close to the heart. This is connected by a light wire to a digital display which can be attached to the rider's wrist or to the pommel of the saddle. This is the most efficient and convenient method.

The first requirement is to be aware of the animal's pulse rate at rest in the stable, and again when he is tacked up and taken out into the yard ready for work. It will be between 36 and 42 beats per minute when he is at rest, and will go up to perhaps 40 to 46 when he is tacked up and taken out. After periods of work in his interval training the pulse may rise to 80–100 beats per minute; if it goes over 100 he is probably not fit enough for the task in hand. If he *is* fit enough, the pulse should return to around 60 after 2–3 minutes at walk.

The next requirement is to find a suitable training area. It is most convenient if the track used is a circuit so that the horse and rider return to the trainer at the end of each period of work and rest, in order that pulse rates can be taken. Also, if the work can be done slightly uphill, the pace can be reduced whilst the amount of effort required remains the same. Work on the flat, or worse still, downhill, increases the jarring and consequently the risk of concussion-related injury. In any case the going should be good: a sandy track is good in most weather conditions; hard or stony going should be avoided for fear of jarring or bruising; and deep going should never be used for fear of pulling tendons or wrenching joints. It is useful if a number of training areas are available, as horses soon learn to anticipate where they are going to gallop if the same area is used all the time.

When calculating the amount of work that should be done – how far, how fast, and the pace at which the horse should be worked – it is necessary to return to the original aim of his training. The ultimate objective is to prepare the horse to gallop over the competition distance plus 50 per cent. This is based on the assumption that the effort required to jump a cross-country fence at a gallop, is equal to galloping 200 metres at competition speed on the flat.

The aim for the horse under consideration is 'To prepare him for an Intermediate horse trial in three months time'. The requirement of an Intermediate horse trial is that he should gallop a cross-country course of between 2,400–3,620 metres (2,622–3,960 yards/1½–2¼ miles) at 570 metres (623 yards) per minute. If his first competition is to be over an average Intermediate course of 3,000 metres (2 miles) the aim is to train him to gallop 4,500 metres (2¾ miles) at 570 (623 yards) per minute.

CONDITIONING

WEEK 1

Daily routine: to start with, give 3/4 hour ridden work at walk in the morning. Road work is acceptable as it helps to harden the legs, but only if it is safe and fairly free from dangerous traffic. Otherwise work on softer going, off the road is preferable. The walk must be active but unhurried, and on a long rein where possible. As his fitness improves the horse can be asked to walk on, up into the bridle rather more, and taking a contact. In the afternoon, he will be led out in hand for 1/2 hour.

Check carefully for any signs of rubbing, or girth galls.

WEEK 2

As for week 1. Increase the morning work to 1–1 1/2 hours. Introduce some slow trotting 2–3 minutes at a time, preferably on a slight rise, but not downhill as this may cause strain on the tendons, ligaments and joints of the unfit horse. The work should be carried out with a rein contact but not fully 'on the bit'.

WEEK 3

As for week 2. Increase the morning work to 1 1/2 hours. This may be 50 per cent trotting, fairly steadily, preferably up a slight hill, and with a rein contact. The walk should be a good marching pace, coming onto the bit.

WEEK 4

As for week 3. Increase the morning work to 2 hours. Increase the trot work to 75 per cent of the total. In his trotting sessions he should now be working more onto the bit.

Towards the end of this week include 20 minutes lungeing in the afternoon. The circle should not be too small, not less than 18 metres (19 1/2 yards), and the side-reins should be adjusted so that the horse can take a contact with the bit.

HARDENING-UP

WEEK 5

Begin to change from Horse and Pony cubes to perhaps a 'hunter mix' with a slightly higher protein content. Horse and Pony cubes are about 11 per cent protein, some 'hunter mixes' are 12 per cent. Increase the concentrate/fibre ratio to 60/40 per cent.

Increase the morning work to 2 hours. Walk the first and last mile to ensure that the horse is given adequate time to warm up and cool down.

The ridden work should now include some school work in the indoor school or outdoor menage. This will be aimed at improving the medium walk, the working trot and, if he is ready, the working canter.

Some leg-yielding, 20-metre circles, progressive transitions and trotting-pole work can be included. The outdoor ridden work will now include some slow canters.

The following is a suggested programme to incorporate interval training in week 5 of the training programme:

Monday

Walk the first mile.
Trot 5 minutes on the bit.
Walk 3 minutes on a long rein.
Trot 5 minutes on the bit.
Walk 3 minutes on a long rein.
Trot 5 minutes on the bit.
30 minutes schooling.
30 minutes hack out, walking the last mile.

Tuesday

Increase trotting periods to four lots of 5 minutes.
30 minutes schooling over trotting poles and gridwork.
30 minutes hacking out. Include variety ie walking and trotting through water, walk up and down some steep slopes, cross some small ditches, include some light canter work.

Wednesday

30 minutes schooling, improving basic paces rhythm and tempo. Include progressive transitions, some lengthening of the steps in trot, leg-yielding in walk and trot, 20-metre circles reducing to 15 metres and returning 20 metres. Schooling in free walk on a long rein. Improve the work through the corners in trot.
1 hour hacking as on Tuesday.

Thursday

Walk the first mile.
Three 5-minute periods of trotting on the bit with 3-minute rests at walk on a long rein.
Mark out a 570-metre track which is suitable for cantering. Canter over it at a steady pace that suits the horse at this stage in his training, starting the stopwatch as he crosses the start and stopping it as he crosses the finish. Note the time taken. Eventually he will be required to cover this distance in a minute, and later keep that pace up over a course of about 3,500 metres.
Walk for 3 minutes on a long rein.
Canter the 570-metre track once more at a steady canter, again recording the time.
1 hour hacking as on Tuesday.

Friday

Walk the first mile.
30 minutes schooling over trotting poles and gridwork from trot.
1 hour hacking. Include some light canter work and as much variety as possible.

Saturday

Walk the first mile.
Three periods of trotting for 5 minutes with 3-minute rest periods.
Mark out a 700-metre track, with a check marker at 350 metres and canter it steadily aiming at 2 minutes (350 metres per minute). Take and record the pulse rate at the start and finish, walk for 3 minutes and repeat the exercise. Total cantering 1,450 metres.
1 hour hacking as on Friday.

WEEK 6

Sunday

Rest day.
Lead the horse out in hand or, weather permitting, turn him out into the field in a New Zealand rug.
Feed a bran mash. Reduce concentrate in diet by 50 per cent. Increase hay to a full net all day.

Monday

30 minutes quiet schooling on the flat.
Three periods of trot for 5 minutes with 3-minute rest periods at walk.
Two 3-minute canters at 350 metres per minute, with 3 minutes rest at walk in between. Total cantering 2,100 metres.
When cantering in interval training ask the horse to canter on a little over the last 30 seconds or so of each canter period. His willingness to do so will give an indication as to whether or not one is asking too little or too much. During the last half minute of the rest period check his pulse. If it has returned to normal the length of the next rest period should be reduced.

To improve his fitness the horse must be working under some stress. If the pulse is allowed to return to normal he will not be working hard enough to make progress.
30 minute hack out.

Tuesday

1 hour hack out.
30-minute schooling on flat.

20-minute gymnastic schooling over cavaletti and small show jumps.

Wednesday
Three periods of 5 minutes trotting on the bit with 3 minutes active walk rest periods. Pace judgement training: mark out a 400-metre canter track

and try to canter it in 1 minute. Three minutes rest at walk, then repeat the canter exercise. Take pulse rate at start and finish of each canter exercise. 30 minutes varied schooling. 1 hour hacking out.

Thursday
As for Tuesday.

Friday
30 minutes hacking out. Three periods of 5-minute trotting with 3-minute rest periods. Trotting on the bit and, if possible, on an uphill gradient. Three periods of canter for 3 minutes at 350 metres per minute pace; 3-minute rest periods at walk; take pulse rate

at the start and finish of each canter exercise. Total cantering distance 3,150 metres. 30 minute hack out.

Saturday
Compete in novice dressage competition.

WEEK 7

Sunday
Rest day. Carry out normal rest-day routine.
Start 'strapping', as distinct from just grooming

Monday to Saturday
As for week 6. If during the interval training the pulse rate is returning towards normal the rest periods may be reduced to 2½ or 2 minutes; the work

periods should remain the same. The shortening of the rest periods must be at the trainer's discretion. For example, if the horse is blowing excessively or is distressed in

any way the rest periods should not be reduced, they may even be extended. The object, is gradually to reduce them as the horse becomes fitter and is able to cope with a greater workload.

WEEK 8

As for week 7.
Monday's schooling on the flat may now include asking for more engagement and submission in the working paces and direct transitions. Some

work in shoulder-in will help with suppleness and engagement of the hind legs. The trot circles may be reduced to 10 metres. Some practice in riding the dressage tests used in

Intermediate horse trials can be started here.
Tuesday's jumping may include gymnastic training involving showjumps and beginning to school round a small course.

On Saturday a local indoor show may be available with a couple of suitable jumping classes, not more than .90m (3ft), to quietly start off his competition jumping.

CONDITIONING THE HORSE'S WIND

WEEK 9

Start to increase concentrate/fibre ration of the diet to 70/30 per cent

Sunday
Normal rest day.

Monday
1½–2 hours hack out. Give variety, hillwork, ditches, small jumps (a fallen log in the woods), work in and out of water, light relaxed cantering, practise dressage work (leg-yielding, lengthening the steps, serpentines, simple changes, turn on the forehand, rein-back etc.)

Tuesday
Hack out ½ hour.
Three lots of 5-minute trotting with a 2-minute rest periods. Three 800-metre canters at 400 metres per minute, with 3-minute rest periods in between. Total 2,400 metres. ½ hour relaxed walk home.

Wednesday
40 minutes dressage training to include all the work required in the Intermediate horse trial dressage tests.
30 minutes gymnastic jumping training.
1 hour hack out.

Thursday
1 hour hack out as on Monday. 40 minutes cross-country jump schooling round a novice course: schooling over the fences individually, perhaps putting three or four fences together as a course to finish up.
½ hour relaxed hack home.

Friday
40 minutes dressage training as on Wednesday.
20 minutes trotting poles and low cavaletti work.
½ hour relaxed hack home.

Saturday
½ hour hack out.
Three periods of 5 minutes trotting with 2-minute rest periods in walk, on the bit and if possible up a slight hill.
Four periods of canter 800 metres at 400 metres per minute with 2½ minute rest periods at walk. Total canter 3,200 metres. Take note of the pulse rate at start and finish of each canter session. If the pulse rate is returning well towards normal, the canter work can be lengthened the following week.

WEEK 10

Sunday
Normal rest-day programme.

Monday
Hack out 1½–2 hours, working on dressage, jumping and gymnastic exercises where possible. Hacking must always be useful, productive work.

Tuesday
½ hour hack out to warm up. Two 800-metre canters at 400 metres per minute.

Two 800-metre canters at 500 metres per minute. Total cantering 3,200 metres.
½ hour hack out to relax and cool down.

Wednesday
20 minutes dressage schooling.
40 minutes gymnastic jumping training, including some show jumps at .90 metre (3ft). The maximum height for show jumps in an Intermediate stan-

dard horse trial is 1.20 metres (3ft 11in). Include a double of 1.7 metres (3ft 6in) uprights at about 7.5 metres (24ft 6in). 1 hour hack out.

Thursday
20 minutes warm-up in walk and trot.
Three 800-metre canters at 400 metres per minute.
One 800-metre canter at 570 metres per minute (competi-

tion pace). Total cantering 3,200 metres.
½ hour relaxing hack home.

Friday
45 minutes schooling over cross-country jumps.
1½ hours hack out.

Saturday
Compete in 2,000 metre (1½ mile) novice hunter trial at ¾ pace.

WEEK 11
Two weeks to go to first competition

Sunday
Normal rest day. Walk out in hand for an hour, having competed on Saturday.

Monday
1¹/2 hour hack out
20 minutes light schooling on the flat.

Tuesday
1 hour hack out.
³/4 hour gymnastic work and showjumping schooling.

Wednesday
¹/2-hour warm-up in walk and trot.

Gallop three 3-minute periods at 400 metres per minute. Total galloping 3,600 metres.
¹/2 hour relaxing hack back home.

Thursday
2 hours hack out.

Friday
40 minutes dressage training.
20 minutes gymnastic training.
1 hour hack out.

Saturday
45 minutes schooling over cross-country course.

WEEK 12
Final week before first competition

Monday
¹/2-hour warm-up in walk and trot.
Gallop two 3-minute periods at 400 metres per minute, with 2-minute rest periods at walk.
Gallop one 3¹/2-minute period at 570 metres per minute. Total galloping 4,400 metres. (Remember the aim is to train the horse to gallop 4,500 metres at 570 metres per minute.)

Tuesday
¹/2-hour warm-up in walk and trot.
40 minutes dressage training.
30 minutes showjumping.

Wednesday
¹/2-hour warm-up in walk and trot.
Gallop one 5-minute period at 400 metres per minute.
5-minute break in walk.

Gallop 5 minutes at 400 metres per minute and 1 minute at 570 metres per minute. Total galloping 4,500 metres.
5-minute break in walk.
Gallop, uphill, ¹/4 mile starting at 500 metres per minute and finishing as fast as he wants to gallop, giving plenty of space to slow down gradually. This 'pipe-opener' gives the lungs an opportunity to expand to their fullest extent for one short burst.
¹/2 hour quiet hack home.

Thursday
1¹/2 hours quiet hack.

Friday
Light exercise, some dressage schooling, gymnastic jumping exercise.

Saturday
First one-day event.

RETENTION OF CONDITION OVER COMPETITION SEASON

WEEK 13

Sunday
Normal rest day.
Lead out in hand for ¹/2 hour.

Monday to Friday
Relaxed hacking out for 1¹/2 to 2 hours per day.

Maintaining fitness and enthusiasm over an eight- to twelve-week competition season is as demanding on the trainer/rider as the initial fittening and training period. Careful monitoring of the animal's physical condition and mental attitude is important; as far as his physical condition and mental attitude is important; as far as his physical condition is concerned; the normal signs of well-being are a good indication as to whether all is as it should be:

1 The horse should remain relaxed and good natured. Changes in personality may indicate that he is going stale.

2 He should continue to be well covered with muscle, and should have a soft shiny coat, the skin remaining supple and moving freely over the underlying tissues.

3 The stance at rest should be normal, with no sign of resting a forelimb excessively.

4 The appetite must continue to be good.

5 The passing of dung and urine must remain normal.

6 The mucous membranes of the eyes, nostrils and mouth should remain a salmon pink colour.

7 Monitor temperature, pulse and respiration rates regularly and record them. Any noticeable variation from normal may be a sign that all is not well.

8 When at work, a loss of natural enthusiasm to gallop, a loss of natural impulsion in his work, or a tendency to avoid or refuse a jump are serious signs that he is, for some reason, beginning to resent what he is being asked to do.

9 Unwillingness to load into a horsebox or trailer, which is a change in character, may indicate a loss of enthusiasm for competition.
Most horses know where they are going when they are plaited up, dressed in their travelling equipment and loaded into a box.

WEEK 14

Sunday
Normal rest day.

Monday to Saturday
Return to the normal training programme. The date of the next competition will already have been decided so the programme can be worked backwards from that date.
The horse is now thoroughly fit and will have benefited from a gallop over a full competition cross-country course. It now remains to keep him fresh and keen over the competition season. Experience has shown that there are various considerations that will help to achieve this:

1 Reduce the stamina work and continue the periods of fast work.

2 Vary the training area.

3 Avoid any opportunity for the horse to become bored.

4 Avoid overlong periods of schooling in the dressage arena. A 20-minute session is usually sufficient.

5 Loose jumping makes a change.

6 Turn the horse out to grass as much as possible.

7 Keep the diet appetising without spoiling the nutritional content.

8 Take the horse hunting in the winter months if he has become really stale.

LIBRARY
BISHOP BURTON COLLEGE
BEVERLEY HU17 8QG

FOUR

BASIC TRAINING OF THE COMPETITION HORSE

The child that is taught to be literate and numerate, to have basic good manners and that is helped to physical fitness, is better placed to take a useful, productive place in society than the child that is deprived of this basic training. The same principles apply to the horse. If his attitude to life is established in the early years, he should make a willing partner whose co-operation and generosity will make him a pleasure to ride for another fifteen years or so.

Apart from studying his breeding, it is difficult to assess his potential as a competition horse until he begins to mature. The conformation of the foal may give encouraging or discouraging indications as to what his eventual mature conformation will be, but it is not until maturity, at about four years old, that final decisions can be made.

To avoid confusion once training starts, the trainer should decide, in clear terms, what his aims are. Then in those times of difficulty which are sure to arise he can refer to his initial aim, and this will often guide him to the answer to the problem. The aim of the basic training of any riding horse is to put the horse in a position where he can improve his own basic paces and his own natural outline whilst carrying a rider on his back. To enable him to do this he must:

1 | Submit to the trainer's/rider's wishes.

2 | Go forward both physically and mentally.

3 | Be calm and confident.

4 | Learn to walk, trot and canter in balance.

The young horse's training must be progressive. He is usually a willing pupil provided that he is not confused, unable to understand what is required of him, or being asked to do something of which he is incapable. A, B and C must be well established if D, E and F are to follow. If A, B and C are not established, D, E and F may be impossible, or at the very best, of inferior quality.

THE HORSE'S BEHAVIOUR AND NATURAL INSTINCTS

It is important for the trainer to study the horse's natural instincts so that he can employ them to his advantage and ensure that the horse does not use them to the trainer's disadvantage.

In very broad terms the horse responds to two types of situation: those that he finds pleasant, and those that he finds unpleasant. The trainer can use this to his own advantage by employing the principle of 'the association of ideas'. That is, when the horse responds and does something that he is required to do, he is rewarded by a congratulatory word and a pat on the neck. When he does something that he is not permitted to do he is immediately reprimanded with a 'growl' from the trainer and perhaps a slap with the whip. The cause and effect must coincide exactly if the principle is to be successful.

The herd instinct in the horse is very strong and can be used to advantage, since where a trained horse will go an untrained horse may often follow – into water, over a ditch or down a steep slope.

The horse has acute senses and very quick reactions, and his natural response to being hurt or frightened is to run away. It is this natural ability and willingness to get up onto his toes and run that makes him so suitable a subject to train to gallop and jump. Developing and guiding this natural ability is a fundamental part of training a competition horse.

● **Fig 18** The handling of the foal in the early stages may have an effect on all his future training

As soon as he is foaled the young horse's training should begin. Initially he must develop a relationship with his dam, and this should not be interrupted by any human implanting himself as the parent; but nonetheless, the earlier the foal gets used to human company the better. In the first two days he must be patted and stroked, and handled generally with a firm but gentle approach; a foal slip might be fitted. At the first opportunity after 48 hours, weather permitting, he should be turned out to grass with his dam for an hour or two. The mare will be led out first in a head collar, and the foal will follow in a foal slip; one person is required to lead the mare and another to guide the foal. He must be guided by the foal slip, but he is urged forward by an arm being put round behind his hind quarters – he must never be pulled by the foal slip. In any case, he will have a strong urge to follow his dam. Being led in hand is an important part of his early training, and the sooner he lets himself be led willingly from both sides, the better. Mature horses that are difficult to lead because they pull or hang back are tiresome, and this fault may affect other aspects of their training.

It is a good plan to put a coloured jumping pole on the ground across the gateway into the field: the foal will soon step over this without noticing it as he follows his mother out each day. This simple effort may save a lot of time and energy at a later date when work on ground poles is started.

In his first few weeks he should learn to have his feet picked up, his mane and tail handled, his body lightly brushed, and his nose, eyes and dock sponged; he must learn, too, to follow his dam into a lorry or trailer. Later he must have his feet trimmed by the farrier. The bigger and stronger he gets before these tasks are carried out the more likely he may be to resist.

It is an advantage to show him at an early stage, first at foot with his dam, and later in-hand as a yearling and a two-year-old. Any experience that he can be given in public, or at a show, will help to give him confidence and establish good manners.

A common problem often encountered when training mature horses is that they are one-sided, or stiff on one rein. In many cases they are stiff to the right, but are seldom stiff to the left. A contributory factor to this stiffness to the right may be that trainers have a tendency to do most things from the near side (the left-hand side) of the horse. They lead from the left, tack up from the left, start grooming on the left-hand side, and put the rugs on from the left, all of which tend to encourage the horse to look a little to his left. If all these tasks were carried out evenly from both the left- *and* the right-hand side, the horse would stand a better chance of maturing without a positive stiffness to any one particular side.

At some time in his first year he might be introduced to wearing a stable rug, and later a New Zealand rug. Accepting a roller is a useful introduction to fitting a saddle, which will come in two years' time.

If he is to be shown in hand, as a yearling and as a two-year-old, he must learn to accept a thorough grooming. Throughout his first, second and third year this general handling and introduction to the world should continue. He should be encouraged to be confident in the company of human beings, though he must *not* be allowed to be over-familiar. Tit-bits as a reward should be avoided as they may eventually lead to the horse expecting them, and it is then only a short step to him beginning to nip or bite.

As a rule his backing starts at three years old. The aim of this is to lunge him until he responds to the basic words of command, accepts the saddle and bridle, and allows the rider to mount and ride him away quietly in walk and trot. Tactful lungeing also builds up a degree of physical fitness and strength, which helps him to carry a rider complete with saddle and bridle. This is 'backing' as distinct from 'breaking-in', in which the horse is forced to accept the rider.

Lungeing techniques are discussed in chapter 8.

When the horse will lunge quietly and accepts the saddle and bridle, the rider can be introduced; a lightweight, competent rider is required who is supple and agile and who will develop a sympathetic understanding with the young horse. The popular image of a tough, cowboy-type rider who will cling onto a bucking young horse until it submits, does not conform to the principles of correct, classical horsemanship. If the horse objects to the rider by bucking or resisting in some other way, a fault has been made somewhere in the preparatory training.

On the day that the rider is to be introduced, it is best if the work can be done in an indoor school or a small paddock. To start with, the horse is fitted with his saddle and bridle and is lunged in the normal way, on both reins, for sufficient time for him to settle and be paying attention. The trainer then coils up the lunge-rein and stands at the horse's head where he can pat him and talk to him. The side-reins are disconnected and the stirrups and leathers removed from the saddle. The rider stands at the saddle, on the near-side, pats the horse on the neck and pats the saddle on the flaps on both sides and on the seat. He may put one hand on the pommel, the other on the cantle and move the saddle about a little, just to let the horse know that something will be happening in the saddle area. This procedure is then repeated on the off-side.

At this stage it is quite helpful to have an assistant: he can now give the rider a leg-up, on the near-side to begin with, so that the rider lies across the saddle; he should keep his body low all the time, and should pat the horse on the off-side shoulder. If all goes well the exercise can be repeated on the off-side. During this work the trainer stands at the horse's head, talking to him and patting him on the neck.

This is all that need be attempted on the first day. On the second day, the first day's training is repeated; if all goes well, the horse can be walked forwards for five or six steps with the rider lying across the saddle, and if he does so calmly and halts when he is asked to do so, he must be rewarded. The exercise should be repeated on the off-side; and the day's work can then be concluded. If difficulties are encountered it may be necessary to go back to confirm a previous stage. To make progress, both trainer and rider must be firm and persistent, but calm and sympathetic.

When the horse will allow himself to be led quietly in walk, with the rider lying across the saddle from either side, he is ready for the rider to be legged up carefully so he can sit in the saddle. At this stage it is a sensible precaution to fit the horse with a neck-strap in case of emergencies. Once mounted, the rider should keep his upper-body low, close to the horse's neck, to avoid causing alarm. The horse is then led forwards a few paces in walk. If all goes well and he walks on calmly, the rider can gradually bring his body to the upright

● **Fig 19** Showing the young competition horse in-hand is an important part of his early training

position. It is not possible to make accurate generalisations as to how long this will take, but suffice it to say that this stage must not be rushed, and that progress should be made as and when the horse shows that he is ready.

When he can be led in walk with the rider in the saddle, the stirrups can be returned and the rider can begin to take up the reins. The next stage is for the trainer to lead the horse forwards using the voice aids, whilst the rider tactfully applies the leg and hand aids in unison with the trainer's voice. Eventually the rider takes over both the voice, leg and hand aids whilst the trainer continues to lead. This can be developed into trot for short periods, the rider sitting at first and later, if the horse is calm, rising.

As work progresses, the trainer should soon be able to lead the horse at walk, trot and to change the rein with no problems, and he can then begin to let the lunge rein out so that the horse is working on a circle – about 16- to 20-metres (17-22yd) diameter is the eventual aim. The rider now becomes more responsible for the aids, aiming to take over completely from the trainer. When the horse will walk, trot, walk from trot and halt from the rider's voice, leg and hand aids, the lunge rein can be disconnected and he can work on his own. If working in an arena the rider should now go large, making frequent changes of rein and progressive transitions. At this stage the importance of rewarding the horse when he does well cannot be over-emphasised.

The next stage is for him to work in a more open area, perhaps a large field, although in the initial stages this should be a field that he knows well.

This would conclude the horse's backing as a three-year-old, and he would be turned away for a year to mature. At four years old he would be brought in again, and his three-year-old work confirmed before his serious ridden work was started.

FIVE

TRAINING THE DRESSAGE HORSE

WHAT IS THE JUDGE LOOKING FOR?

The rules for both national and international dressage are clearly laid down, and it is the responsibility of judges and competitors alike to study and understand these rules. The rules for jumping leave little, if any, room for discussion: a show-jump pole that is knocked down is, in all but the most obscure circumstances, clear for all to see and there can be no argument about the judges' decision. But in dressage, the judge must interpret the rules in the spirit in which they are made and award a mark for each movement which is in effect his *own* opinion, formed by his interpretation of the rules. Clearly, judges' opinions will vary from time to time, a factor that competitors must learn to understand and accept.

Some dressage rules are easier to interpret than others. For instance the rules for dressage above novice level require that 'The horse in all his work, even at halt, shall be on the bit'. If he is not on the bit for all, or the main part, of a particular movement the best mark that he can be awarded is 4. However, opinions between judges may of course vary in what constitutes being 'on the bit' for a particular horse.

In all his work the horse must 'go forward'. In riding the horse this means more than just proceeding in a forward direction by putting one foot in front of the other. Whilst he must be progressing physically forward he must be going 'mentally' forward as well.

The rules also require that the horse shall be 'submissive'. This does not mean that the horse is broken in spirit with no personality or character of his own. What it does mean is that he works without resistance and tries his best to carry out his rider's instructions. Any sign of resistance – refusing to go forward with enthusiasm, swinging the hind quarters to the left or the right, hollowing the back, coming above the bit, dropping behind the bit, swishing the tail or grinding the teeth – all these will be penalised by the judge.

The horse must be 'straight': that is, his body must follow the straightness of straight lines, and be bent throughout its length (as far as is anatomically possible) on the curve of a corner, turn or circle. Horses that are unable to show straightness or a uniform bend on a turn or circle will be penalised for being stiff, or resistant, or both.

He must work in a regular tempo appropriate to each of the three paces, and must maintain it on the straight, through the corners, on turns and circles and in lateral work. Variation in tempo caused through loss of balance or disobedience will be penalised.

The transitions from one pace to another must be good. A good transition is one in which one good quality pace becomes another without hesitation, resistance or loss of balance or form.

Accuracy is most important, and the judge expects the test to be ridden exactly as the written test-sheet demands. Where a movement or change of pace is required at a given marker it

• **Fig 20** This young horse is soft, submissive and going forward

should be made as the rider's shoulder passes that marker. Inaccuracies will be penalised if they are due to carelessness or ineffective riding on the part of the rider, or disobedience on the part of the horse. However, in a novice test, a young horse which makes a good transition a metre before the specified marker is unlikely to be heavily penalised.

The school figures, turns, pirouettes, transitions from one pace to another, transitions within the paces, and lateral work, are all designed to show how well the basic paces are established. Deterioration of the pace whilst executing any of the work required in the dressage test will be penalised. For instance the walk pirouette is designed to show off the horse's suppleness and balance in walk. If, in the execution of a walk pirouette, the true four-time rhythm is lost, the movement will be penalised.

ESTABLISHING THE BASIC PACES

All the work in the dressage test, from 20-metre circles in working trot right up to piaffe and passage

in extreme collection, is designed to demonstrate the quality of the horse's basic paces whilst carrying a rider. It therefore follows that if these paces are not well established initially, a) the more advanced work required in the tests will be difficult to achieve, and b) the work will never be sufficiently correct to score good marks.

Some horses are blessed with naturally elegant paces, some have moderate natural paces and others have poor paces. Clearly those with natural ability are very rewarding to train, but all horses, no matter what their natural ability, can be improved to some extent. Improving the balance, suppleness and agility of a horse with limited natural talent can be as rewarding as improving a naturally gifted horse.

The quality of the paces is affected from the day his training starts. It is vital that in the early stages the trainer and rider have a thorough understanding of what is required in walk, trot and canter.

● **Fig 21** A good, natural walk is important to the competition horse

Faults created by carelessness or ignorance in the early stages may be very difficult to rectify later in the training. If, for instance, the walk has been shortened in the early stages by bad riding or the use of some mechanical aid which pulls the horse's head down and in, that shortened walk may be very difficult to improve when medium and extended walk are required. Any technique employed in the early stages that forces or even encourages the horse to carry himself in an outline for which he is neither physically nor mentally ready may create lasting difficulties.

Each individual pace has its own rhythm, which is the number of beats in one full stride. This will be covered later in the discussion of the individual paces. Rhythm should not be confused with 'tempo' which, in training the horse, means the speed of the rhythm. The tempo should remain constant throughout his work whether it is on the straight, through the corner, on a turn or circle or in lateral work, in collected, medium and extended paces. Unintentional variations in tempo will be penalised by the judge.

ESTABLISHING THE WALK

The walk is perhaps the most difficult pace to improve and the easiest to spoil. For various reasons it is often neglected – for example, it is the pace used to give the horse a rest between periods of work, so the rider tends to lose concentration himself and allows the horse to walk incorrectly; it becomes hollow, or fails to continue to walk 'forward' with energy. This encourages the horse to think that a poor walk is, at times, acceptable, which it is not. It is quite possible to allow the horse to rest at walk without abandoning the basic principles of walking correctly. Again, there are some riders who think of the walk as a pace less exciting than trot or canter, and consequently devote less time and enthusiasm to working at its improvement. In fact the establishment of the forward impulse in walk requires greater equestrian skill than at trot or canter. Unskilled schooling at walk frequently shortens or hurries the steps, and this detracts from the correctness of the pace.

The walk is a pace in four-time in which the feet come to the ground in the following order: outside hind, outside fore, inside hind, inside fore. The steady, repeated, four-time rhythm is essential in all work at this pace. For instance, the half-pirouette in walk will be severely penalised if the four-time rhythm is spoilt in its execution.

Four types of walk are required in the various dressage tests: collected, medium, extended, and the free walk on a long rein; and there are basic qualities that are required in all types of walk:

1   The four-time rhythm should remain constant and even.

2   The steps should be long, deliberate, generous, even, regular, and marching.

3   The horse should walk using his whole body: thus the head, neck, shoulder, elbow, knee, back, loins, croup, hip, stifle, hock and tail should all move. The horse that walks from the elbow and the stifle downwards, with the rest of the body remaining stationary, is walking badly, like the mule or the donkey. The head and the neck should swing up and down, in rhythm with the stride, and this must not be discouraged by the fixed hands and elbows of the rider. In walk, the horse moves each of his four legs individually, and his back swings up and down and from side to side. This swing of the back must not be restricted by a rider who is stiff in the back himself, or finds it difficult to let his seat swing in unison with the swing of the horse's back. The tail should hang in a relaxed manner, and swing softly with the swing in the horse's back – a clamped-down tail or a tail held stiffly to one side is a sure sign of stiffness or tension.

4   It is sometimes said that the horse should over-track in walk, ie the foot-print made by the hind foot should be in advance of the foot-print made by the forefoot on the same side. This is indeed an indication that the steps are generous. However, in the long-backed horse (some mares are long in the loins to facilitate the carrying of a foal) the walk may be good but with little over-tracking due to the conformation. This lack of over-tracking should not be penalised if the other aspects of the walk are good.

Riding the horse in walk

A considerable part of the competition horse's work will be done in walk; at least part of the warming-up programme and most of the cooling-down programme will be in walk. Whilst maximum energy and impulsion will not be required under either of these conditions, the basic qualities that constitute a good walk must not be overlooked. Common faults include walking in a hollow outline, above the bit: this should not be permitted. Some horses develop the irritating habit of jogging when being asked to walk with energy: this must not be permitted, either. A horse must be reprimanded when he jogs, and brought back to walk.

The horse that has a naturally easy, swinging walk is a pleasure to ride, but all are not gifted in this way. Developing the walk is often helped if the horse is worked in company with another that walks out well. Walking uphill on good going is an advantage; walking downhill on deep or slippery going is a disadvantage. Continued training in walk in an indoor school or enclosed manege may in fact discourage some horses from walking generously; although some training under these conditions is at some point essential.

To achieve a good walk, the normal aids to ask the horse to go forwards should be applied, ie closing both legs just behind the girth and allowing the horse to walk forward by 'giving' with the hands. The leg aids can be reinforced by a touch with the whip if and when required. The practice of using left and right alternate leg aids in rhythm with the stride should be discouraged, as it tends to make the animal 'dead to the leg' – horses soon learn to ignore repeated aids for which the rider does not insist upon a response.

Improving the walk requires feel and understanding on the part of the rider. The horse must be allowed to swing his head and neck in rhythm with the stride. A rider with stiff, set hands and elbows discourages the swing of the head and neck, and spoils the walk; the rider with a soft elbow and shoulder allows his hand and forearm to move with the swing of the horse's head and neck and thus encourages a good walk. The rider who is stiff in the back discourages the horse from swinging his back, and consequently spoils the walk. To improve the horse's walk, it is important for the rider to blend the swing of his hips into the swing of

● **Fig 22** Medium walk. Here the steps are long, generous, even and regular

the horse's back, without making more movement than the horse makes for him.

Achieving collection in walk involves the same principles as in the other paces. It consists of slowing down the speed by the use of the half-halt (see p60), whilst maintaining or increasing the impulsion by the use of the leg aids. This clearly has a potential for increasing undesirable tension in the horse and must only be attempted when the horse is mentally and physically able to cope with it. It is best achieved by experimentation. Little by little the request for collection is made, and whilst the horse remains relaxed and submissive the work can continue. When resistance and tension are encountered the work should be discontinued until submission and relaxation are re-established, when the attempts to achieve more collection can be resumed. Submission and relaxation must remain the prime considerations.

Medium walk

Medium walk (see Fig 22) is the easiest walk for the horse because it is closest to his natural walk. The term 'working' (as used in other paces) is deliberately avoided when referring to the walk, as it tends to infer short or over-busy steps.

Collected walk

In collected walk, the major joints in the hind leg (the hip, stifle and hock) show maximum flexion, enabling the hind feet to come well underneath the horse thereby lowering the croup and raising and lightening the forehand. This in turn means the steps become rounder and more elevated, giving increased mobility. In collection the horse remains submissive, relaxed and on the bit, with the front of the face approaching the vertical. The neck is raised and arched.

Extended walk

In extended walk the horse shows great impulsion and takes steps of maximum length. The steps remain unhurried with an unaltered tempo, but the speed increases as more ground is being covered with each step.

'Free walk on a long rein'

'Free walk on a long rein' (see Fig 23): here the horse is given the opportunity to take the maximum amount of rein, and is encouraged to stretch the head and neck forward and down. The rider maintains a light contact on the mouth through the reins and the bit. The steps remain long, deliberate and even.

Improving any pace depends on creating impulsion without resistance, developing suppleness and agility, and rewarding the horse when he does well. There are many exercises that help to instil these qualities – leg-yielding, transitions from one pace to another, gymnastic training using ground poles, turns and circles and gymnastic jumping – all these improve agility, co-ordination, suppleness and gymnastic ability, provided they are used tactfully (ie when the horse is ready and the exercises are appropriate) and that the horse continues to enjoy his work.

Variety is an important element in every aspect of the horse's training. It can be boring to work day after day in the same surroundings and to repeat the same exercises continually. Much of the work that is done in the riding school can equally well be done whilst out hacking: lengthening the steps, leg-yielding and turns and circles can be practised to very good effect in suitable areas on a cross-country ride.

ESTABLISHING THE TROT

The trot is the pace in which most of the competition horse's training will be carried out. It is important therefore, that both the rider and the trainer have a clear understanding of what is required in the trot work of a dressage test, and how the horse should work in trot in his general training. In the dressage test, four types of trot are required: collected (Fig 25), working (Fig 24), medium (Fig 26) and extended (Fig 27).

● **Fig 23** Free walk on a long rein. The horse should take as much rein as possible

LIBRARY 51
BISHOP BURTON COLLEGE
BEVERLEY HU17 8QG

The trot is a pace in two-time in which the horse springs lightly from one diagonal pair of feet to the other, with a period of suspension, when no feet are on the ground, between the diagonal pairs. As in all paces, some horses are gifted with an elegant, cadenced trot, whilst many others are less fortunate; but as in all the work, careful and intelligent training can improve even the least talented horses. It must be repeated that a well balanced rider who applies the aids with 'feel' will be most successful in improving the trot. The work in rising trot is important in that much of the fittening work will be done in this pace. The rider who is unable to rise correctly and who causes the horse discomfort in this work will not improve the trot. Likewise the stiff or unbalanced rider who gives the horse a difficult load to carry in sitting trot will be unable to develop the trot work that will be required for a good mark in the dressage tests.

Collected trot

The French term for 'collection' or '*to collect*' is rather more descriptive than the English: it is *rassembler*, meaning 'to gather together' or 'to muster'. The rules require that, as in all his work, the horse remains on the bit. There is great flexion of the joints of the hind leg, which lowers the croup and lightens the forehand, making the horse light and mobile. The forehand is able to move freely in any direction. The neck is raised and arched, the front of the face approaching the vertical. The steps are round and mobile, covering less ground than the other trot steps.

Collection is achieved by slowing the speed over the ground and increasing the impulsion. An advanced demonstration of this is shown in piaffe where the speed is reduced to zero but the horse, with great impulsion, continues to trot on the spot, remaining relaxed and confident without resistance. Good collection can only be achieved by

• **Fig 24** Collected trot

skilled, tactful riding. If an increase in collection is insisted upon by the rider/trainer before the horse is physically or mentally ready, tension and resistance are sure to ensue. If the horse is not physically ready, the increased muscular effort required for collection will result in physical discomfort and tiredness, and this will detract from his willingness to co-operate. If he is not mentally ready, the increase in impulsion combined with the requirement to slow the pace may build up tension that creates undesirable results.

Collection is achieved mainly by the use of the half-halt: the leg aids are used to encourage the horse to work energetically forward, whilst the fingers of the outside hand ask him to relax his neck, poll and jaw and to slow the speed. It is an area of training in which the feel and imagination of the rider are of great importance. The rider who asks too much will create resistance; the rider who asks too little will achieve nothing.

For the horse to be mentally ready for this work he must be confident and trusting, supple, strong and well co-ordinated. There are many exercises that will help to achieve these qualities: correctly ridden transitions from one pace to another help the horse to establish his balance and co-ordination; correctly ridden turns and circles improve supple-

ness; the turn on the forehand and leg-yielding improve co-ordination; work in shoulder-in improves the flexion of the joints of the hind legs, increasing engagement.

Working in collection is essentially an area of the horse's training in which he must remain in 'self-carriage', and where pulling, leaning on the bit or dropping behind the bit are all serious faults.

Working trot

This is described in the dressage rules as 'the pace between collected and medium trot'. It is, however, the pace at which the horse will carry out most of his ridden training. He must be 'on the bit', supple and relaxed, and working with good hock action. In the competition dressage test the judge will expect a slight degree of collection in 'working trot' that the rider will probably not ask for in the horse's day-to-day trot work.

Establishing working trot is achieved by the rider being conscious of the requirement of a correct, natural trot ie good forward impulsion, relaxation, acceptance of the bit, regular tempo and being ridden between the leg and hand.

● **Fig 26** Medium trot

Medium trot

The requirement for medium trot is a pace in between working and extended trot. By the time the horse reaches the stage where he is required to show medium trot he will have been asked in the tests to 'show a few lengthened steps', and these can only be achieved correctly if they are made from a slight degree of collection. The spring cannot be released until it has been wound up. When lengthened steps are required in the novice tests they are usually shown as faster, running steps on the forehand, and this must result in a poor mark. In fact they can only be made from a slight increase in collection – only then can the horse spring effortlessly into longer steps when asked to do so from an 'allowing' hand. More impulsion is required for extension (longer steps) than for collection (shorter steps). The same principle must be employed for training towards medium trot: when

a degree of collection can be achieved without resistance, medium steps can be asked for by allowing the head and neck to be stretched forward and down a little, and an increase in stride length asked for by effective use of the leg aids. The horse remains on the bit and between the leg and hand.

Flicking out the forelegs with a pointed toe is not showing medium trot: medium trot is shown by good flexion of the hip, stifle and hock joints, the hind legs stepping well under the body and a corresponding lengthening of the steps made by the forelegs. The tempo remains the same, as in collected and working trot. An increase in the tempo invariably means that the horse is running and not lengthening correctly.

Extended trot

In this pace as much ground as possible is covered with each step. The tempo remains the same as in the other types of trot, but the steps are of maximum length as a result of great impulsion from the hind legs. Each foot is placed on the ground at the spot at which the toe is pointed. The same principles are employed to achieve extended trot as for medium trot, but the horse must be sufficiently well prepared to remain calm and in balance whilst coping with the maximum impulsion required for extension. Once again it is for the rider, through practice and experimentation, to ask with his legs for the required impulsion and to allow the horse to extend by exactly the right amount of 'allowing' and 'restraining' in the hands.

In all this work the trainer on the ground can tell the rider what he is doing and what he ought to be doing, but in the end it is the feel and imagination of the rider that instills the impulsion and balance in the horse. Lengthening the steps comes easily to many high-couraged horses that are blessed with natural impulsion, provided that they can cope mentally with the work. However, in horses which do not have naturally athletic conformation, or are not endowed with natural impulsion, high quality extension may be very difficult to achieve.

ESTABLISHING THE CANTER

Canter, developing into gallop, is a most important pace for the competition horse. Most of his competition jumping will be from canter or gallop, so if the jumping is to be good, the canter and gallop must be good.

Canter is a pace in three-time in which the feet come to the ground in the following sequence: outside hind, inside hind and outside fore together, inside fore, followed by a period of suspension when no feet at all are on the ground. After this period of suspension the stride is restarted with the outside hind.

The qualities of a good canter are similar to those in other paces. The horse must remain supple, relaxed, obedient, on the bit and in self-carriage, being light in the hand. In showjumping and cross-country riding, however, the rider expects to have more weight in the hand in canter than in the

• **Fig 27** Extended trot

● **Fig 28** Collected canter. The outside hind leg can clearly be seen starting the canter stride

dressage test – it gives a rider confidence when jumping to have what is sometimes referred to as a 'healthy feel' in the hand, with the horse accelerating into his fences but without pulling.

Four different canters are required in the dressage tests: working, collected (Fig 28), medium and extended.

Collected canter

Collection in canter, as in the other paces, means a shorter and rounder horse with the hind quarters well engaged, the forehand light and mobile, the steps shorter and rounder, and the neck raised and arched. It is achieved by gradually training the horse to increase the impulsion whilst keeping the speed slow. Particularly in canter the horse must remain mentally relaxed in this work, since any tension may result in crookedness (loss of control of the hind quarters), loss of the three-time rhythm, cantering disunited (when the pair of legs that come to the ground together are on the same

side of the horse), changing the leading foreleg, or disobedient flying changes.

Working canter

This is the canter at which the horse naturally works best. Often both horses and riders find that the easiest way to improve this pace is to ride outside with the stirrups two holes shorter, thus allowing the weight to be taken off the horse's back, and to work in a steady hand-canter up a slight slope on good going and on the bit, allowing the horse to find his own balance. Young horses in particular often make better progress under these circumstances than working in the manege or indoor school.

Medium canter

This is described in the rules as the pace between working and extended canter. The horse goes freely forward with the steps moderately extended, the increase in stride length coming from greater engagement of the hind legs, which ensures that the forehand remains light. The steps are unhurried, remaining in the same tempo as collected and working canter. He remains on the bit and is allowed to carry his head a little in front of the vertical, lowering the neck and the head slightly to accommodate the longer steps.

Extended canter

The steps are of maximum length as a result of great impulsion created by the muscles and joints that control the hind legs. It is not galloping, which would be in four-time. The horse must remain light in the forehand, able to make a transition to trot, or back to medium or working canter as required. The speed is greater because the steps are longer, not because the tempo has been increased. He is allowed to carry his head further in front of the vertical, and the neck and head are lowered further to assist in maintaining the balance.

Lengthening the steps to either medium or extended canter must not result in the horse pulling or leaning on the bit. He must remain 'between the leg and the hand'. The half-halt can be used to achieve this in medium and extended paces, just as it is used in working and collected paces.

In all work in which the horse is required to take longer steps – whether it be in walk, trot or canter – he must be allowed to alter his outline to maintain his balance and to have the physical ability to lengthen the steps. It is generally accepted that the balanced horse cannot put his forefoot down on the ground further forward than the tip of his nose – he can *stretch* it further forward, but he must bring it back to put it on the ground. It is doing this which makes the 'toe-flicking' show horse action, but it is not true extension and would be penalised in the dressage test. Effective use of the rider's legs creates greater energy from the hind legs and consequently longer steps from the hind legs. This is the correct start of extension. To allow the forelegs to take correspondingly long steps, the rider must allow the stretching forward and down of the neck and head, otherwise the steps will be tense and restrained. The ability to create energy with the legs and seat, and to receive and guide and control it with the hands, is perhaps the most important skill that the dressage rider must develop. Whilst the trainer can explain what he should be trying to achieve, it is a matter for the rider's 'feel' and imagination and his natural genius as a horseman to extract the best from each individual horse.

● **Fig 29** Working towards collection in canter

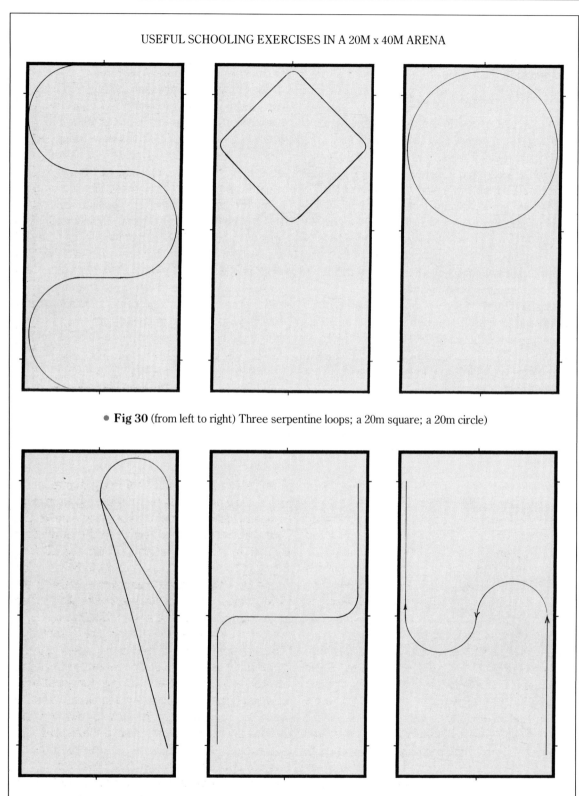

USEFUL SCHOOLING EXERCISES IN A 20M x 40M ARENA

• **Fig 30** (from left to right) Three serpentine loops; a 20m square; a 20m circle)

• **Fig 31** (from left to right) Two versions of changing the rein by half a 10m circle from a quarter marker; changing the rein by turning at the half markers; changing the rein by two half circles through X

USEFUL SCHOOLING EXERCISES IN A 20M x 40M ARENA

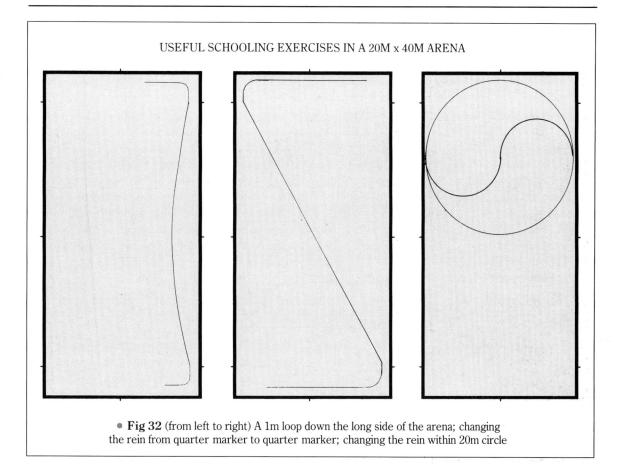

● **Fig 32** (from left to right) A 1m loop down the long side of the arena; changing
the rein from quarter marker to quarter marker; changing the rein within 20m circle

Counter canter

To demonstrate his obedience, suppleness and balance, as the tests progress the horse is required to make 'counter canter', in which he canters on the left rein with the right fore leading or on the right rein with the left fore leading. In competition it is only asked for in collected canter, and all the qualities of the true canter must be maintained. The bend in the horse is in the direction of the leading foreleg, making counter canter one of the very few exercises in which the horse is asked to bend in the opposite direction to which he is going. It must not be confused with incorrect canter in which the horse, by mistake, canters with the wrong foreleg leading. Counter canter should not be attempted until the horse can make working canter on both reins, with relaxed confidence and a degree of collection. The transitions to canter on both reins from walk and trot should be well established. The first attempts should be made on the rein that the horse finds the easiest, as this will discourage any attempt to make a disobedient flying change.

A simple introduction to counter canter is to make a shallow loop along one long side of the arena, about 1 metre in depth, starting at the first quarter marker and finishing at the second (see Fig 32). To start with, the horse can be taken off the track with a slight opening-rein effect with the inside hand. The inside leg remains at the girth to maintain the forward impulsion, the outside leg is taken back towards the canter aid to ensure that the true canter is continued. In this exercise a few steps of introductory counter canter are made as the horse returns to the track from the small loop. He must remain in balance throughout the exercise with the bend towards the leading foreleg. No attempt must be made to change the leading leg. As he progresses in this exercise the loop can be made larger, eventually reaching the centre (A–C) line. Progress should not be hurried and the trainer must be prepared to go back to a smaller loop to re-establish the work should this be necessary. As far as possible the work should be done equally on both reins, but one rein will almost certainly be easier than the other.

When making loops in canter from the long side, care must be taken to ensure that a 'true' loop is made. There is sometimes a tendency for the horse to make a sort of half-pass off the track and to leg-yield back onto the track. This is an evasion, or at least a misunderstanding, and should be avoided. When the counter canter loops can be made in balance, an attempt can be made to ride through a corner in counter canter, perhaps making the corner a quarter of a 10-metre circle, possibly larger but not smaller. From there, counter canter can be attempted around the whole short side. Eventually the horse will be required to make serpentine loops in canter, each loop going to the track on the long side.

Counter canter is an essential requirement for making flying change successfully, and to this end transitions from trot and walk to counter canter should be established. The aids for making counter canter with the right fore leading should be identical to the aids for making true canter right, and the aids for making counter canter with the left fore leading should be identical to the aids for making true canter left. At first, transitions to counter canter should be made on the straight and in the direction of canter that comes most naturally to the horse. Once these transitions have been mastered on both reins on the straight, they should be attempted in the corners. The logical sequence to this is that the horse should be worked on a 20-metre circle in either walk or trot, and asked to make the transition to canter left or right and back again to walk or trot, whilst continuing on the circle. When these transitions can be made confidently and without tension it is usually only a short step to making correct flying change.

The half-halt

The horse's balance, when carrying a rider, is closely related to the speed at which he is travelling and the amount of impulsion with which he is working. 'Speed' and 'impulsion', whilst they are related, are not the same thing. The horse that is trotting fast – on his forehand and on a loose rein, perhaps downhill – is working with little use of the hind legs (impulsion) even though he may be travelling quite quickly. This horse is out of balance because the speed is too great for the impulsion with

which he is working. At the other extreme is the horse that is full of impulsion, the hind legs well engaged, the croup low and the forehand high (perhaps in the starting-stalls at the start of a race); but he is strongly restrained by the rider and is on the verge of rearing up. This horse is out of balance because the impulsion is too great for his speed, which at that moment is zero.

These are two extremes, but the principle applies throughout the whole spectrum of the horse's work. Depending on his stage of training, the speed in miles per hour and the degree of impulsion with which he is working must be complementary to one another. The advanced horse can work in piaffe (trotting on the spot): he has massive impulsion and virtually no forward progress. He is able to do this because he has been carefully trained, over a long period of time, both physically and mentally, to achieve this skill. The young, untrained horse could not cope with working with this amount of impulsion at such a slow pace.

The exercise used to achieve this balance between speed and impulsion is known as the 'half-halt', and is another aspect of riding which is largely dependent on the 'feel' and 'imagination' of the rider. In practice it is a subtle, momentary use of the fingers of the outside hand that say to the horse 'slow down fractionally'; this is in conjunction with the use of the seat and inside leg which say 'but keep energetic'. It is a brief command to keep or regain the horse's attention and/or to keep, adjust or regain the balance. It can be repeated as often as necessary to achieve a result. Where, when and how much it is used is entirely a matter for the rider to decide. The half-halt can be used to great effect before transitions, before and during turns or circles, lengthening of the steps, and any lateral work, to achieve collection, in the approach to a jump, and in almost any other aspect of the horse's training.

LATERAL WORK

Lateral work is work in which the horse steps forwards and sideways at the same time. The ultimate exercise in lateral work that is required in competition is the half-pass which is ridden in trot and canter. The training leading up to half-pass is most beneficial to the horse as it improves his suppleness, balance, co-ordination, agility and submission, and encourages the flexing of the hip, stifle and hock joints, thereby enhancing collection.

Lateral work is usually introduced to the horse, perhaps unwittingly, when he is asked to move over in his box whilst being mucked out. When one side of the box is done the groom will often put his hand on the horse's quarter, give a slight push and say 'over', and the horse crosses his hind feet, one in front of the other, to move across the box.

Leg-yielding

The first ridden lateral work is usually 'leg-yielding' where the horse, not yet ready for collection, is asked, in medium walk and later in working trot, to step forwards and sideways whilst remaining parallel to the side of the arena. The dressage rules require that he should be 'bent at the poll away from the direction in which he is going' (see Fig 33).

In fact this may lead to a horse tilting his nose to the left or right; and the young horse may develop an inclination to look away from the direction in which he is going in more advanced work, which is contrary to the basic principles of training. There appears to be no reason why the horse should not remain quite straight whilst stepping forwards and sideways in this exercise (see Fig 34).

Leg-yielding may first be attempted by making half a 10m (11yd) circle from the quarter marker in walk; on reaching the centre line, whilst keeping the horse quite straight, the rider applies the inside leg just behind the girth, asking him to step sideways a little as well as forwards. If three or four obedient steps are taken he should be rewarded

● **Figs 33-4** Leg-yielding to the left: (left) with a bend to the right; (right) almost straight, but with some nose-tilting to the left

LIBRARY
BISHOP BURTON COLLEGE
BEVERLEY HU17 8QG

● **Fig 35** In leg-yielding, whilst remaining straight or bent at the poll a little away from the direction of movement, the horse steps forwards and sideways in a lateral movement

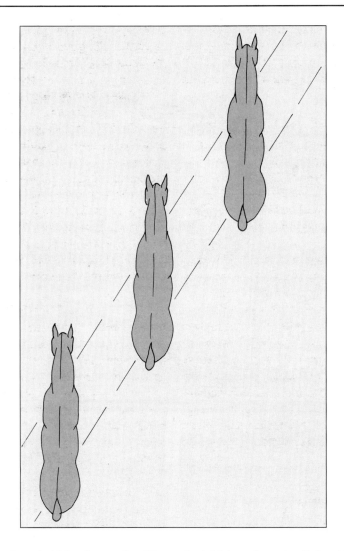

with a pat on the neck and ridden forwards. The horse that is inclined to step sideways too much from the inside leg must be ridden forwards with both legs. The steps in leg-yielding should be as much forwards as they are sideways – never more sideways than forwards.

This exercise is often successfully introduced down the long side of the arena where the forehand is taken off the track half a step to the inside. The horse is kept straight by the use of both legs and equal contact in each hand and is asked to step sideways from the rider's inside leg. After three or four steps of leg-yielding he can be ridden forwards across the diagonal without taking the forehand back onto the track.

Once progress is being made in walk the exercise can be attempted in working trot, usually in sitting trot although some horses and riders find the initial work easier if the rider continues to rise. Invariably the horse finds this work easier in one direction than the other, but as in all his training, he should be made to work equally on both reins. Leg-yielding can be practised whilst out hacking, maybe along a quiet track where circumstances permit. The rider must take care to make clear transitions between going straight and leg-yielding, and leg-yielding and going straight. It is clearly a mistake for the horse to drift in a sideways direction as a result of careless riding.

A similar exercise, sometimes known as 'yielding to the leg', can be ridden on the circle. It is usually started in medium walk; as progress is made, it can be attempted in working trot. The horse is worked on a 20m (22yd) circle which is gradually – about a metre at a time – reduced to a 10m (11yd) circle. Then, keeping the horse bent on the circumference of the circle, the rider closes his inside leg and encourages the horse to step forwards and sideways back out onto the 20m (22yd) circle. As usual the exercise should be carried out on both reins.

The turn on the forehand

The turn on the forehand is a useful exercise in teaching the horse to move away from the leg. From a square halt, on the bit, the horse makes a 180-degree turn pivoting around one forefoot and making a half-circle with his hind feet, the radius of which is the distance between his forefeet and his hind feet.

It is important that the exercise is ridden 'forwards' and that the horse makes no attempt to step backwards – the rider must understand that this is a 'leg-yielding' exercise, made 95 per cent with the legs and only 5 per cent with the hands. To make a turn on the forehand to the right (so that the horse finishes the exercise facing to the right and on the right rein) the fingers of the right hand ask him to look fractionally to the right, the left hand maintaining a contact, ready to discourage him from stepping forwards. The right leg is applied just behind the girth, asking him to step round to the left by

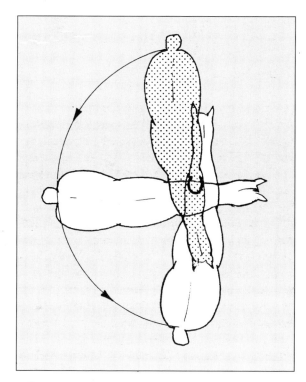

● **Fig 36** Turn on the forehand

crossing over his hind feet. The left leg is kept in contact at the girth, again to discourage him from stepping backwards should he be so inclined. On completion of the 180-degree turn he should be ridden energetically forwards.

The turn on the forehand is a good co-ordinating exercise for both the horse and rider, and should be practised to the left and the right.

In order to ensure that the forward impulse is maintained, this exercise is sometimes ridden as a 'turn about the forehand'. In this case the same exercise is ridden, but from an energetic medium walk instead of from halt. The forefeet walk a small circle instead of pivoting around the inside forefoot, and it is even more important that the regular four-time rhythm of the horse's walk is maintained.

The Shoulder-in

Under normal circumstances, this exercise is the next logical step in training in lateral work. It has many beneficial effects if introduced correctly: like the other exercises, it continues to improve balance, suppleness, co-ordination and submission, and it has further advantages in that it helps with control of the shoulders, and encourages the flexing of the joints of the hind legs thereby lowering the croup and lightening the forehand.

In shoulder-in, the forehand is taken slightly off the track so that the horse is working on three distinct tracks: one track made with the inside forefoot, a second with the outside forefoot and inside hind, and a third track with the outside hind (see Figs 37 and 38). This exercise is required in dressage tests from elementary standard upwards, to demonstrate suppleness, balance and submission. In the tests it is ridden in trot, but in training it can be introduced in walk and is useful as a straightening exercise in canter, qv. It can be used effectively to improve the transition to canter, and as a preparation for riding corners and circles from 10m (11yd) downwards.

In competition, shoulder-in is ridden in collected trot with a bend throughout the length of the horse's body (or as far as is anatomically possible). The degree of bend required progresses with the standard of the test: at elementary level the bend (depending on the horse) should be as for a 10–8m (11–8½yd) circle. The bend required at Grand Prix, however, would be very much more, up to

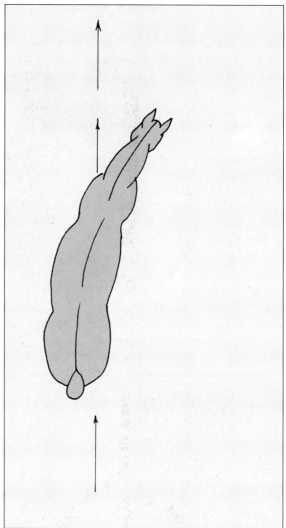

● **Figs 37–8** Shoulder-in on three tracks. In shoulder-in the horse is bent throughout his length in the direction in which he is going. The forehand is taken in from the track so that he is working on three tracks

that required on a 6m (6½yd) volte. The degree of bend demonstrates the suppleness and balance of the horse, and it should not be so exaggerated, at any level, that the quality of the trot is to any degree jeopardised.

Shoulder-in is best introduced to the horse in walk from a 10m (11yd) circle, the walk being a little on the 'collected' side of 'medium'. The circle is made to establish the required degree of bend and is started from a marker to help keep the geometry correct. As the horse returns to the marker at the completion of the circle, he is ridden forwards to take the first step on a second circle.

As that step is made, his progress forwards is lightly checked with the fingers of the outside hand, and the inside leg is applied at the girth to encourage him forwards along the track with the forehand just off the track to the inside. He must remain on the bit, with the correct four-time rhythm of walk maintained. The rider's outside leg remains ready to keep him straight should he attempt to escape by swinging the hind quarters out. If three or four obedient steps are made, he should be rewarded with a pat on the neck and ridden forwards on the circle. This is easier for him, in the early stages, than being brought back onto the track.

To ensure that the forward impulse is maintained, this exercise should be made in trot (a little on the 'collected' side of 'working') as soon as the horse understands what is required in walk.

Travers

Travers is the next stage of training in lateral work (see Figs 39 and 40); it is a quarter controlling exercise closely related to half-pass, in which the forehand continues straight down the track, and the hind quarters are brought in from the track so that the horse is working on three tracks: one track made with the outside forefoot, another with the inside forefoot and the outside hindfoot, and a third with the inside hindfoot. It also has the usual qualities of all lateral exercises, that is, it improves co-ordination, balance, agility, and helps to increase the use of the joints of the hind legs.

Once again it is best introduced in walk, to give both horse and rider time to understand what is required. As soon as this is established, the exercise can be carried out in trot. A practical way of starting this exercise is, once again, from a 10m (11yd) circle (as for shoulder-in). On completion of the circle, just as the horse's nose and ears are pointing straight down the track, the rider's outside leg is

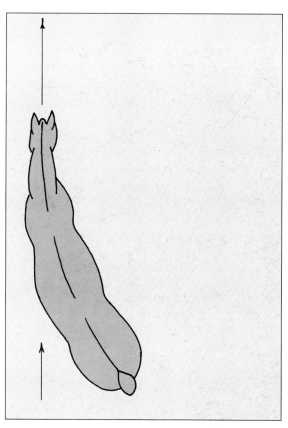

● **Fig 40** In travers the forehand continues straight up the track whilst the hind quarters are brought in a little to form three tracks

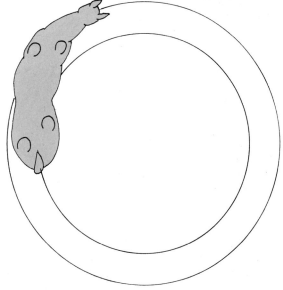

● **Fig 41** Travers on the circle is a supplying exercise in which the forehand makes one circle and the hind quarters are taken in to work on a slightly smaller circle, forming three tracks

● **Fig 39** Travers

65

brought back a little to bring the hind quarters in, just off the track; the inside leg is kept at the girth to maintain the impulsion and to encourage the horse forward, the forefeet continuing straight down the track. The hind feet are brought in and cross over to make the three tracks.

Renvers

This is defined in the rules as 'the inverse movement to travers with the tail instead of the head to the wall' (see Fig 42). Similar principles apply to renvers as to travers, ie the horse is in collection and working on approximately three tracks (outside hind, inside hind and outside fore, and inside fore); the difference is that he is bent away from the direction in which he is working (ie on the right rein he is bent to the left, and vice versa). It is an exercise in suppleness, balance and to test his

readiness to respond to the aids; start in walk, and once this is established it can be taken on into trot. Renvers is usually started by making a half 8-metre (8½yd) circle from the long side; at the end of the half-circle, as the horse's nose and ears are pointing straight up the arena, the rider's outside leg (the leg on the outside of the horse's bend) is brought back to keep the bend and to take the hind quarters onto three tracks, in exactly the same way as travers. After a few steps in renvers he is either ridden straight forwards, or the second half of the 8-metre circle is ridden to take him back onto his original track.

Half-pass

Once shoulder-in and travers have been mastered, half-pass can be attempted (see Figs 43 and 44). This exercise is made in collection in both trot and

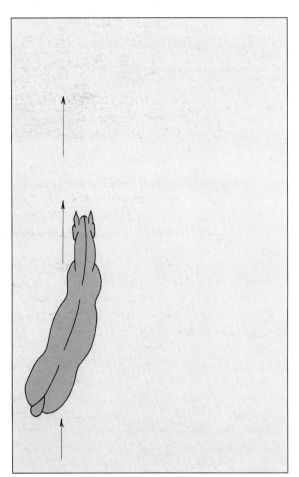

● **Fig 42** Renvers is the movement similar to travers in which the forehand continues straight up the inner track, the hind quarters being taken towards the wall to form three tracks

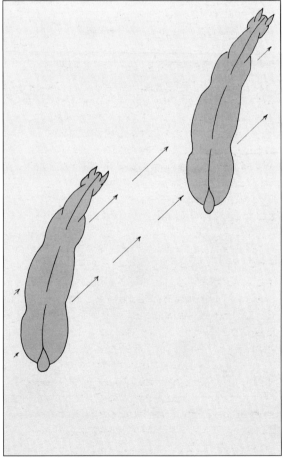

● **Fig 43** In half-pass the horse takes steps forwards and sideways whilst remaining bent, throughout his length, in the direction in which he is going

canter; the horse must maintain a good bend in the direction in which he is going, and takes steps both forwards and sideways to move diagonally across the arena. Ideally he remains almost parallel to the side of the arena, his outside feet crossing in front of the inside feet to achieve the sideways movement; but the steps must be as much forward as they are sideways ones, and the forehand must always be slightly in advance of the hind quarters.

Half-pass can be approached in a number of ways, depending on the horse and his natural aptitude for coping with new demands. In order to give both horse and rider time to understand what they are trying to do, it is – as always – an advantage to start this work in walk.

A 10m (11yd) circle is made, on the easier rein in one corner of the arena; this helps to establish the required bend. It is followed immediately by a 10m (11yd) half-circle, but as the horse reaches the centre line, further progress on the circle is halted by soft checking with the outside rein; the forward impulse is then maintained with the inside leg, the inside hand 'leads' the forehand sideways to the track, and the outside leg, brought generously back, asks for the hind quarters to be taken across towards the track. If a few acceptable steps in half-pass are achieved the horse is patted on the neck and ridden forwards. Eventually as sufficient steps in half-pass are made to return to the track, both legs should be applied to ride him forwards before he reaches the wall.

Alternatively, the exercise can be started by making a 10m (11yd) half-circle from the quarter marker at the end of the track to establish the bend, and as the horse reaches the centre line he is ridden for a few steps, five or six, down the centre line in shoulder-in. He is then in the ideal situation to be asked to make half-pass, by the rider leading the forehand towards the track with the hand, and bringing his outside leg back to move the hind quarters across towards the track.

If both horse and rider are competent in travers, it often proves successful to attempt half-pass by simply riding travers diagonally across the arena from one quarter marker towards the opposite quarter marker. If a few steps are successfully achieved by using this method, the horse should be ridden forwards directly up the arena, and rewarded with a pat on the neck.

Half-pass is also ridden in canter, and comes

● **Fig 44** Half-pass

more easily to some horses at this pace than it does in trot. It can be started from the 10-metre (11yd) circle as described in the trot exercise, or by the third method described above, ie riding travers across the centre line.

Eventually, to demonstrate his balance and agility, the horse is trained to make 'counter change of hand', a set number of steps in half-pass performed on each side of the centre line in a zig-zag manner. It should not be attempted until half-pass, with a good degree of collection, is well established on both reins. It can be usefully attempted by making four or five steps in half-pass (on the more difficult rein) out of the corner from the quarter marker. On completion of these steps the horse is ridden forwards for two or three steps to change the bend and adjust the balance with the half-halt. He should then be ready to make four or five steps in half-pass on the opposite rein, back to the track. Once the horse clearly understands the requirement and as the exercise progresses, the number of straight steps can be reduced until he can change the rein directly in half-pass without tension or loss of balance.

In all lateral work, each exercise should be followed by a period in which the horse is ridden energetically forwards, to ensure that the forward impulse is not allowed to deteriorate due to the sideways nature of these exercises. There are a few common faults that appear in this work, and these are as follows:

1. Insufficient lateral bend is shown in the direction in which the horse is moving. This is sometimes as a result of too much work in careless or incorrect leg-yielding with the neck bent away from the direction of movement. Starting half-pass from a well established 10-metre circle can be very helpful in correcting this fault. It should be used in conjunction with any other suppling exercise that encourages the horse to bend softly in the direction in which he is working.

2. The hind quarters lead the movement. This may be due to poor riding: for example the rider's outside leg is over-used, or the horse is not allowed to go sufficiently forwards. If the hind quarters begin to lead the movement, he should be ridden energetically forwards for a few steps to straighten him, and only then should the exercise be reattempted.

3. The horse goes sideways too much and insufficiently forwards. This may be due to a resistance, loss of balance or poor riding. The most effective correction is usually to ensure that the rider's inside leg is sufficiently effective to keep the horse going forwards. It is a common rider-fault when working in half-pass to concentrate too much on the sideways movement, and neglect the use of the inside leg which is of equal – even greater – importance.

OTHER WORK REQUIRED IN THE DRESSAGE TESTS

The halt

Apart from the entry at 'A', the halt is the first exercise that the judge sees in the dressage test, and may create a lasting impression on him. Some serious attention should therefore be paid to the

• **Fig 45** A good, square halt

way in which it is carried out. The requirement is that the horse shall halt at the designated spot, square, straight and with equal weight on each of his four legs (see Fig 45). He must be attentive and on the bit. The halt should be made directly from trot or canter, as the test directs – unless it specifically states that downward transitions may be progressive. The more common faults are these: that he resists into the transition, coming above the bit; that the halt is not straight; that one leg is rested; that he stands unbalanced (too close or too wide either behind or in front); or that he is inattentive – above the bit and looking around, even whinnying at the other horses. All these would be marked down by the judge.

The transition to halt should be made like any other transition: it should be preceded by sufficient half-halts to ensure that both the speed and impulsion are correct for the transition to be made accurately. As he approaches the spot at which the halt is to be made, the rider lowers the seat softly down into the saddle, closes with both legs to ensure sufficient engagement of the hind legs result-ing in the lightening of the forehand, and asks the horse to halt by a minimum feel with the fingers. Whilst the horse is at halt he must remain on the bit and between the leg and hand. The rider must therefore maintain the rein contact when he puts both reins in one hand to salute, and must keep both legs on the horse's sides. Only in this way will the horse's attention be maintained, enabling him to make a good transition from halt into the next pace required once the salute is completed.

Rider mistakes are invariably the reason for poor halting. These mistakes include: insufficient preparation for the transition – attempting to halt with the horse on the forehand, or above the bit; failing to use the legs effectively and relying only on the hands to ask for the halt, pushing the lower leg forwards and pulling with both hands when asking for halt; and failing to sit still and balanced whilst at halt – often riders can be seen making quite vigorous adjustments to the seat whilst sitting at halt to salute.

In competition dressage a salute is made to the judges, at halt, both at the beginning and at the end of a test. The way the salute is made often has an effect on the halt, which is why it is appropriate to refer to it here. To salute correctly, first take both reins and the whip in one hand (preferably the left): ladies should then bow – from the neck, not the waist; men should remove the hat with the right hand, and lower it to the side – no bowing is neces-sary. The salute should be made elegantly and briefly, but without undue haste.

The simple change of leg at canter

In this exercise the horse changes from one canter lead to the other through two, or at the most three steps in walk, the transitions being directly from canter to walk and from walk to canter. This is the 'simple change' in its most advanced form. To work up to this, the more elementary tests allow for the downward transition to be progressive, ie through trot to walk, though the upward transition to canter is direct. In essence this is a simple test of making transitions and the normal rules apply: the horse must move smoothly, without interruption, from one good quality pace to another whilst main-taining submission, balance and obedience.

Training for this exercise is conducted in pro-gressive stages, and the first step is to work in

canter, changing the rein across the long diagonal from quarter marker to quarter marker. Then across the diagonal line, smooth transitions are made: from canter to working trot, from working trot to medium walk, and after five or six steps, up again to working trot, and once more to canter, preferably all on the diagonal line before reaching the track and the quarter marker. The next step is to reduce the number of trot steps until the walk to canter transition can be made; then to reduce the number of trot steps until the canter to walk transi-tion can be achieved. When a true simple change can be achieved with only two or three steps in walk, then clearly progress is being made, and it is but a short step towards flying change.

The flying change of leg

In this exercise the horse springs lightly from one canter lead to the other without loss of balance, submission or tempo. It is a perfectly natural movement required not only in the dressage test but by cross-country horses, show jumpers and polo ponies alike. In the dressage test it is made in a collected canter, and the change of leading leg is made after the period of suspension which comes at the end of each correct, complete canter stride. After the period of suspension it is one of the hind legs that starts the new stride: if the left hind leg is put down first, the right foreleg will lead; if the right hind leg is put down first, the left foreleg will lead. The rider can tell the horse which hind leg to put down first by indicating with the leg aid and fractionally changing the bend in the horse. If the horse has been taught to canter from a light outside leg aid, it should be fairly simple for the rider to change the bend and ask for the new canter lead just before or during the period of suspension.

It is most profitable if the rider can be taught to make flying change on a 'schoolmaster' horse that is skilled in this work, because he is then in a much stronger position to teach it to a novice horse. There are a number of ways to introduce this exer-cise to the horse, and the method used should be the one that best suits that particular horse, or the one that the trainer/rider has previously used with most success.

A skilled advanced rider may have trained a par-ticularly talented horse to a degree in canter at which he can, whilst working in or towards col-lected canter, ask the horse to make a flying

LIBRARY
BISHOP BURTON COLLEGE
BEVERLEY HU17 8QG

● **Fig 46** Flying change

change. This is often successful, particularly with show jumpers or polo players. However, it requires skill and experience, and if attempted by the less skilled or inexperienced it may create faults that are difficult to rectify.

The first method that may be attempted is to work from quarter marker to quarter marker in canter, in exactly the same way as when training for the simple change. The number of walk steps is reduced until the transition can be made directly from canter left to canter right, or vice versa. The change should be made on the straight line, and *not* as the horse goes through the corner, or at the change of rein: making the change in the corner may be effective, but it introduces an element of initiative – disobedience – in that the horse changes leg due to a loss of balance. It may even cause him to change in front only and become disunited, which should be avoided. The requirement is that he should make the change because he is asked to, and not because he is made to through loss of balance. Invariably most horses find that flying change is easier to accomplish on one rein than the

other – very seldom are they exactly even on both reins. In view of this, it is advisable to attempt to make the changes at first from the more difficult canter lead to the easier one, in the hope that the horse will *want* to change to his easier side. This is particularly so if he is being asked to change from counter canter on his more difficult rein to true canter on his easier rein.

The first, and most desirable method may prove to be too ambitious if employed by a rider with little or no experience of teaching flying change and who is attempting to teach this work to an inexperienced horse. This sort of partnership is frequently found in competition training, and is one which the trainer must learn to cope with. The second method is similar to the first, but the canter is maintained until the horse has arrived at the second quarter marker, at the end of the long diagonal, and is approaching the corner in counter canter. It is often helpful here to tell the rider to ride 'as though he was in sitting trot', and as he rides through the corner to apply the aids exactly as he would if he were asking for canter from trot. If the aids have been consistently and correctly applied by the rider, and have been accepted by the horse, this method is often successful.

The third method is to work on a 20-metre (22yd) circle, making at first trot to canter or counter canter transitions, and canter or counter canter to trot transitions; and later, walk to canter or counter canter, and canter or counter canter to walk transitions. This exercise should be built up gradually, over a period of weeks, to ensure that the horse does not become tense because the demands of the work increase too quickly. Once these transitions can be made willingly and without tension, with perhaps a 20m (22yd) half-circle between each transition, the number of walk steps between canters can be gradually reduced until the horse is ready to make flying change directly from one canter lead to the other. It is usually an advantage to ask at first from counter canter on the least preferred leg to true canter on the leg that he finds easier. The advantage of this method is that the horse is being asked to change his canter lead entirely by the correct use of the aids: there is no reliance on either a change of direction, or the horse feeling that there is a *logical* place to change the lead, both of which introduce an element of disobedience. This means that the rider has an

unlimited number of opportunities to ask for the change, and he can give the aid when he thinks that the horse is ready, rather than at any particular point in the arena.

This work is best started early in the training period, after the normal warm-up work but before the horse begins to tire. Because it is the type of work that may build up tension, it should not be continued for too long. Once even slight progress has been made, the horse should be rewarded with a pat and a short break, after which the training subject should be changed.

Once the flying change is established in both directions, dressage tests will require 'tempo changes': these are flying changes after every four strides, then every three strides, then two strides, and a change at every stride.

The rein-back

All horses must be trained to step backwards when required to do so. It is essential when opening gates out hacking, or perhaps when making way for hounds when out hunting, and for the polo pony under many circumstances. However, the rein-back as required in the dressage test must conform

to clearly defined rules, and the horse must step backwards with diagonal pairs of legs, in a clear two-time rhythm. Each pair of legs must be lifted clearly from the ground without dragging or shuffling, and be put cleanly down, the fore foot fractionally in advance of the hind. It should be made from a square halt, the horse remaining on the bit and between the leg and hand. The dressage test sometimes requires that the rein-back should be immediately followed by trot or canter: under these circumstances the last step in rein-back must be followed immediately by the first trot or canter step – he must not show a sustained halt, nor must the upward transition be progressive.

Serious faults frequently seen in this exercise include resistance whereby the horse comes above the bit, and/or opens the mouth; failing to step back in a straight line, ie the quarters move to the left or the right; the feet being dragged along the ground, and not picked up sufficiently; spreading or inactive hind legs; irregular stride length; and noticeable deviation from the two-time rhythm.

Whilst this is an exercise in stepping to the rear, it must essentially be ridden forwards. The aids are very similar to those for riding forwards to walk from halt, ie both legs are applied at the girth and the horse is allowed to walk forwards from an 'allowing' hand. To rein-back, the same leg aids are applied but, by a tactful feeling from the fingers of the outside hand, the horse is instructed to step backwards rather than forwards. He is not pulled back by the reins and bit, and any attempt on the part of the rider to do this should be discouraged by the trainer. In the initial stages of teaching this exercise, two steps are the most that should be attempted, after which the horse should be rewarded and ridden energetically forwards. As his confidence and understanding of the work improves, more steps can be asked for. This is a demanding exercise putting physical strain on the spine, joints and muscles together with a certain amount of psychological pressure. It should be built up gradually, six steps being the most that are ever required under normal circumstances.

Rein-back can be used as a useful remedial exercise. In circumstances where the horse becomes too strong in his work by leaning on the bit, perhaps in jumping training at canter, he can be brought back to halt and asked to rein-back a few steps to re-establish his balance and submission. Rein-back when used in this way must, of course, be correct, and *not* used simply as a way to pull the horse backwards, as is sometimes seen.

The half-pirouette in walk

The half-pirouette is a turn made through 180 degrees, where the forefeet make a half-circle round the hind feet which make the smallest possible circle, almost pivoting around the inside foot which must nevertheless be picked up and put down in the regular four-time of walk. The horse remains on the bit, and bent a little in the direction in which he is going. The exercise must essentially be made forwards; stepping backwards or sideways will be penalised by the judge, as will any deviation from the true four-time of walk.

To perform this exercise well, a degree of collection must have been developed in the walk. It is an advantage to start with a quarter-pirouette, and to walk energetically forward on its completion, and for the sake of accuracy it is best to start at a marker, having made the necessary half-halts be-

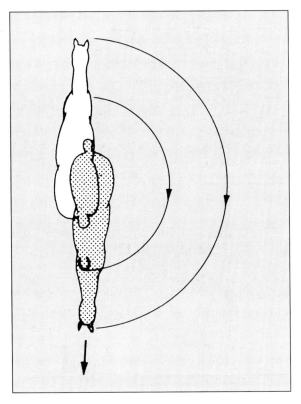

• **Fig 48** Half-pirouette in walk

forehand to ensure an appropriate degree of impulsion and collection. The half-pirouette can be started with a slight opening effect of the inside rein to guide the horse round in the required direction for the appropriate number of steps. The inside leg maintains the forward impulsion and helps with the bend; the outside leg is ready to be drawn back to control the quarters should this be necessary. The rider remains upright, sitting in the bottom of the saddle, with equal weight on each seat-bone, leaning neither to the left nor to the right. Initially, so as to avoid any possibility of stepping backwards, the circle made with the hind feet can be about a metre in diameter. As the exercise improves, this circle can be made smaller, provided that it is not at the expense of forward movement or the true four-time of the walk. Eventually the half-pirouette can be made, at the end of which the horse is walked energetically forward.

Stroking the horse's neck
(Giving and re-taking the reins)

This exercise is required in some dressage tests to show that the horse is in self-carriage, ie that he is not being held up by the rider's hands through the reins and the bit. It is asked for either along one long side of the arena, or across the long diagonal. The rider is required to push both hands forwards, up the horse's neck, so that both reins are released and then re-taken; the horse should continue in a balanced canter, and not snatch his head down when the reins are released. It is not an extended exercise and should be made in one continuous movement. Giving and re-taking the reins should be included at frequent intervals at all paces during the horse's training.

DEALING WITH EVASIONS AND RESISTANCES

Horses, broadly speaking, respond to two types of situation: those that they find pleasant, and those that they find unpleasant. If they are treated firmly, but calmly and with consideration, they respond likewise. If, on the other hand, they are bullied and compelled to do something which they find very difficult or do not understand, they tend to resist or evade what they are being asked to do. Sometimes evasions and resistances are brought about by the horse's temperament or conformational difficulties, but most often they are the result of poor riding or because of counter-productive training techniques.

Crookedness

The horse that goes crookedly (the hind feet not following the same line of tracks as the forefeet) may do so either because he is particularly stiff on one rein; or because he cannot cope with what he is being asked to do and consequently finds an easy way out. This is sometimes brought about by the rider who drives the horse forward with the seat, legs and spurs but does not allow him to go forward sufficiently with the hands. In these circumstances the horse, unable yet to flex the hip, stifle and hock joints to bring the hind legs straight underneath him, takes an easier route by stepping sideways with the hind feet. It is often noticeable in canter where the hind quarters are brought in and the horse is clearly on three tracks. The first remedial exercise is to check that the balance between the leg and the hand is good, and is not causing the resistance. The second is to ride the horse a little towards shoulder-in, bringing the forehand frac-

tionally off the track; this can be done in walk, trot or canter, and whilst straightening the horse, its suppling effect may help towards a permanent cure. The third is to work generally on suppling exercises, turns, circles, serpentines etc, to get the horse sufficiently laterally supple to be able to go straight.

Opening the mouth or crossing the jaw

The horse will sometimes do this to avoid accepting the bit correctly and relaxing the great muscles that control the neck, the poll and the jaw. Some will try at the same time to get the tongue over the bit, an evasion which is very difficult to rectify and often returns in times of stress. Overbitting is a common cause. The horse that is fitted with a drop, flash or crossed noseband and a fulmer cheek snaffle from an early stage in his training, is discouraged from developing these evasions. He must not be prevented from opening his mouth at all, but just discouraged from opening it so wide that it becomes an evasion. These arguments presuppose that he has no other problems in the mouth that cause him to open it, such as wolf teeth, sharp molar teeth, cutting tushes, lampas etc.

Tilting the head

This is the evasion where the head is tipped at the poll so that the nose goes one way and the ears the other. As the horse comes up the centre line it is a very noticeable fault for the judge, sitting at 'C', who will conclude that either the horse is very stiff on one rein, or that the rider is stronger in, or more active with, one hand than the other. The first thing the trainer must do is therefore check that the rider works with even weight in each hand, with reins of equal length, and that the hands are carried as a level pair. Sometimes attempts are made to overcome this evasion by fitting a bit-guard with bristles on the inside, on the side to which the nose is tilted. This may have some superficial effect, but it is treating the symptom rather than finding and relieving the cause.

Swishing the tail and grinding the teeth

These are both resistances that denote tension, and will be penalised by the dressage judge. They are both, usually, reflections of the horse's temperament and his attitude to what he is being asked to do. The swishing tail may be a sign of a lazy

● **Fig 49** This horse is overbent, ie the poll has ceased to be the highest point of the horse – the crest is higher

horse being made to work. Other than ensuring that he is not physically stressed or being caused pain by the work he is being asked to do – he may be suffering from a heavy worm burden, or back-ache or a sore mouth – the only cure is to devise a way that will help him to enjoy his work more. It may be more profitable to work him outside, rather than in an indoor school – he may be bored with working in an arena; most of his dressage training can be carried out, to a degree, whilst out hacking. Hunting, jumping and regular pipe-openers may all help the horse that is troubled with this problem. Finally veterinary advice can be helpful: a horse that is suffering from a vitamin or mineral defi-ciency may well be reluctant to work, and an appropriate additive to his diet (on veterinary re-commendation) may bring about some relief.

Grinding the teeth initially starts as a resistance, but may well develop into a habit which can then be very difficult to cure. It is usually a sign of tension and anxiety brought about because the horse is being subjected to physical and mental pressure for which he is not ready. Teeth grinding is more often found in the Thoroughbred type of horse than the heavier types. Stress may well be a contributing factor.

Overbending

This is an evasion where the poll ceases to be the highest part of the horse and the crest, at some point, becomes higher (except in the case of some high-crested stallions). The front of the face comes behind the vertical. It may be combined with the mouth coming open and the bit being dropped in an attempt to avoid bit contact on the bars of the mouth. This fault is often brought about by severe bitting, schooling martingales or poor hands; if this is the case, changing to a milder bit and being more 'allowing' with the hands is often an effective cure. At times overbending is related to lack of hind leg engagement and being on the forehand; under these circumstances softening the hands and being more effective with the legs often has rewarding results.

TRAINING FOR SHOWJUMPING

Before discussing the technicalities of training the showjumping horse, it is as well to understand the aims and objectives of the showjumping course-builder. His first consideration should be to set a course that will place the best horse and rider combination first. However, his second responsibility is to produce an exciting competition, round an attractive course, to entertain the spectators.

The simplest option when designing a course is to build a straightforward track with fences up to the maximum height allowed by the rules for that particular competition, and to raise the fences substantially in the jump-off. However, this will probably result in only a small percentage of the entry jumping clear, and some of the less talented horses being overfaced, a situation which is bad for showjumping as a sport and is not good entertainment for spectators. Timed competitions around a straightforward course are exciting for the crowd but can result in the class becoming a race, which may eventually spoil some potentially good horses since it invites them to 'hot up'.

The course designer may, on occasions, include a fence which by its siting is difficult to get at: this introduces an element of luck, however, and is not generally thought to be good course-building. Some fences may be built with less 'knock resistance' than others, perhaps using a lightweight top pole on flattish cups. However, this may unfairly penalise some bold horses.

At times 'problem distances' are set in doubles or combination fences; but it is to be hoped that these will *never* be included in novice classes, as it is a serious mistake to test a novice in this way. Even in advanced classes, only a slight variation from 'true' distances (see Fig 50) should ever be included within combinations in a showjumping course.

In general, therefore, the course should test horsemanship and training: it should encourage bold, fluent jumping on the part of the horse, and accuracy and judgement on the part of the rider. The best courses are those that encourage the horse to flow on at an even pace without abrupt changes of pace or direction (see Figs 51 and 52).

The main quality required of a showjumping horse is that he should be bold enough to make a brave attempt to jump any fence his rider sets him at. He must also have a strong sense of self-preservation and an intense dislike of hitting the jumps with his feet, legs or knees; some horses have a natural technique of tucking up both the fore feet and the hind feet to avoid touching a top pole, and these are the most rewarding to train as showjumpers. The horse that is naturally careless and does not mind hitting a top pole is probably not a good one to train as a showjumper. There are a number of exercises and training techniques that may help these horses, but their scope is usually limited.

To quote Reiner Klimke, Olympic and World Champion: 'A jump over an obstacle is simply a longer, higher canter stride'.

The precision required to be successful in the showjumping ring is at least equal to that required in the dressage arena. The only exception to this is that an unskilled rider with a bold, honest horse may well jump clear showjumping; an unskilled rider cannot possibly, however, show the horse off at his best in the dressage arena no matter how genuine the horse.

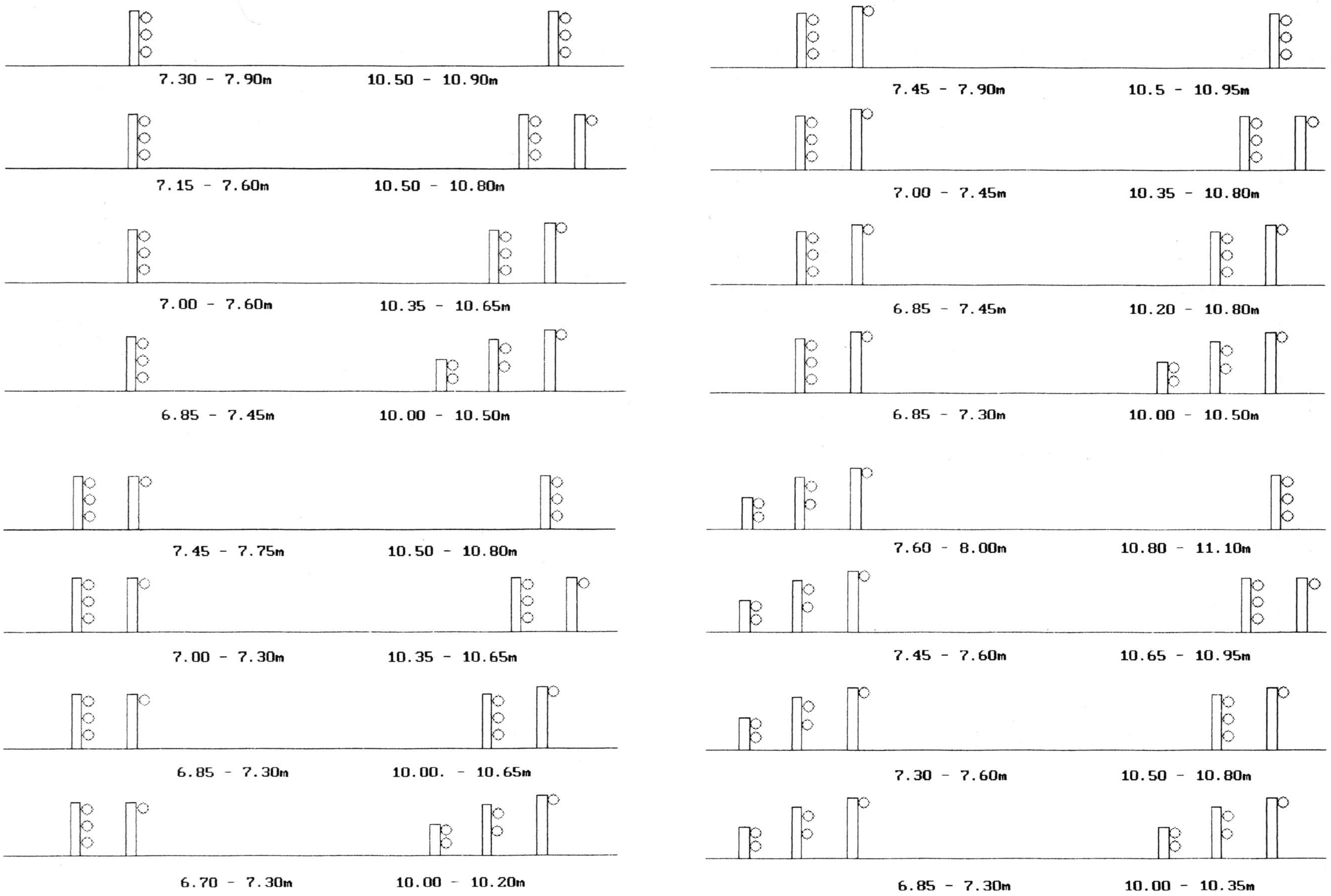

10.5 – 10.95m

10.35 – 10.80m

10.20 – 10.80m

10.00 – 10.50m

10.80 – 11.10m

10.65 – 10.95m

10.50 – 10.80m

10.00 – 10.35m

7.45 – 7.90m

7.00 – 7.45m

6.85 – 7.45m

6.85 – 7.30m

7.60 – 8.00m

7.45 – 7.60m

7.30 – 7.60m

6.85 – 7.30m

10.50 – 10.90m

10.50 – 10.80m

10.35 – 10.65m

10.00 – 10.50m

10.50 – 10.80m

10.35 – 10.65m

10.00. – 10.65m

10.00 – 10.20m

7.30 – 7.90m

7.15 – 7.60m

7.00 – 7.60m

6.85 – 7.45m

7.45 – 7.75m

7.00 – 7.30m

6.85 – 7.30m

6.70 – 7.30m

● **Fig 50** Competition distances in doubles and combination fences

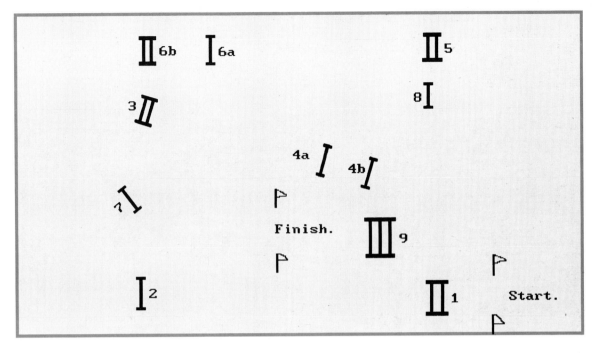

● **Fig 51** A novice horse trial show jumpingcourse. Length 400m; speed 320m per minute; time allowed 1 min 15 secs

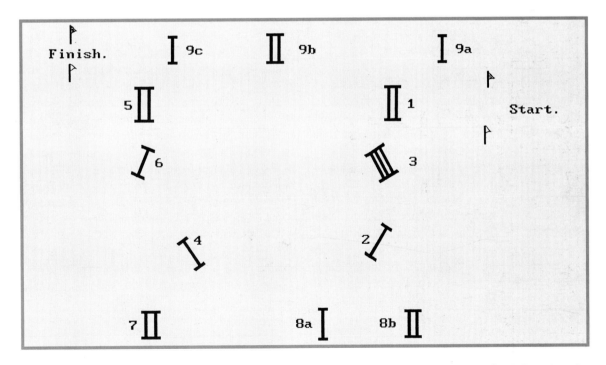

● **Fig 52** A complex and demanding Grade B track set indoors in a 70m x 30m arena. Distance 390m; speed 350m per minute; time allowed 1 min 7 secs

LIBRARY
BISHOP BURTON COLLEGE
BEVERLEY HU17 8QG

● **Fig 53** Good style over a parallel oxer

Developing the qualities required of a show-jumping horse is skilled work for a sympathetic, competent, knowledgeable rider. This horse must be, above all, confident – confident that what he is being asked to do is within his capabilities. Any lack of confidence will result in the horse running out or refusing. He requires the physical qualities of strength, suppleness, balance and co-ordination. His walk, trot, canter and gallop must be well established. He must be able to work on the bit with good engagement of the hind legs resulting in good mobility of the forehand. The absence of any of these qualities makes turning, speeding up, slowing down, or the lengthening and shortening of his stride difficult, if not impossible.

The showjumping horse, like the dressage horse, must be submissive and free from re-sistances: pulling, coming above the bit, dropping behind the bit or working in a hollow outline are all resistances which will detract from his optimum performance. The establishment of the qualities required in the horse is best achieved by progres-

sive, intelligent work on the flat, combined with gymnastic exercises both mounted and dis-mounted. The most important factor is that the work is progressive and that the horse is never asked to go on to work for which he is clearly not ready, due to the absence of one of the qualities previously mentioned. Whilst he must be progres-sively tested, and confronted with new challenges, the trainer/rider must be quick to spot when this progress is more than he can cope with, resulting in a loss of confidence, and perhaps even resistance.

The showjumper must possess the qualities of the middle-distance runner – able to maintain a strong steady pace over about 800m; the sprinter – capable of short bursts of speed; and the gymnast's strength, co-ordination and agility that enable him to jump high and wide. If a showjumper is to work at his best, he should be able to score at least 'sixes' consistently in a novice dressage test. Less ability than this in his flatwork will make it difficult for the rider to be able to present him at a jump straight, and with exactly the right amount of speed, impulsion and submission. Added to which cantering accurately between the fences on a complicated course, at the speed required by the rules, and within the time limit set by the course designer, will also be difficult.

Showjumpers are certainly seen jumping successfully without these qualities, and sometimes at a high level, but they are now the exception rather than the rule. The obedient, relaxed, confident, well trained jumper will jump higher, gallop faster, turn more quickly and above all, last longer than the horse without these qualities.

jump down the line of fences. Some jumping trainers make this a permanent structure, with facilities to raise and lower the jumps and change their type, and to adjust the distance between the individual fences. However, an adequate jumping lane can be made from ordinary showjump material as shown in Figs 55, 56, 57 and 58.

It is best if the horse is introduced to all this with just one inviting jump in the lane, perhaps a small brush fence well within his ability. It should be

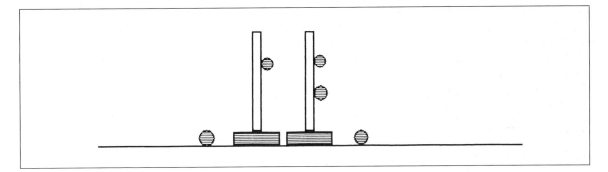

FIRST STEPS IN JUMPING TRAINING

The initial 'introduction to jumping' lesson for any young horse should be on the day that he is first turned out to grass as a foal with his dam: a coloured jumping pole laid on the ground across the gateway into the field will ensure that, following the mare, he will always step over it with confidence. This simple exercise removes the possibility of a confrontation later on. If stepping over a pole is left until he has grown into a strong three-year-old, it is surprising how often such a confrontation occurs.

Jumping training can be approached in three stages: on the lunge, loose jumping, and ridden jumping.

Jumping training on the lunge is covered in Chapter 8.

Loose jumping

Loose jumping is helpful in that it allows the horse to develop his own *natural* jumping technique and find his own *natural* stride without the distraction of carrying a rider. It can be organised in an outdoor manège or an indoor riding-school. Primarily a jumping lane is required – that is, a line of jumps set at distances to suit the particular horse's stride, fenced in so that the horse cannot escape, but must

• **Fig 54** This jump, when included in a gymnastic jumping exercise, will encourage the horse to use his head, neck and back to improve the bascule. The bascule (derived from the French *bascular*, to see-saw), is the shape that the horse makes over a jump when he uses his body efficiently, making a smooth curve from take-off to landing

placed halfway along the lane so that he has sufficient room to approach, and plenty of room after the fence. As he becomes more confident a second jump can be introduced, making the exercise into a double. Upright fences are best for this introductory work, but they should look solid and be inviting. It is important that the distance between these two fences is exactly right for the individual horse, and the type of fence that he is being asked to jump – the recommended distances set for competition doubles and combinations are not always appropriate for schooling exercises. Careful attention must be paid to adjusting the distances so they suit the individual horse in training, and so they take account of any other particular local circumstance such as the type of going or the slope of the ground.

When he has successfully negotiated a double and is making progress in establishing a confident jumping technique, a third and even a fourth jump can be added, until eventually a well-filled spread fence is introduced as the final jump in the lane.

Fig 55 Planks make a solid upright fence

Fig 56 Most showjumping courses include a gate

Fig 57 A spread fence; showjumpers should be schooled over as many different 'fillers' as possible

• **Fig 58** A plain, coloured filler

• **Fig 59** A balustrade filler

• **Fig 60** A double of upright fences at 7.5m

• **Fig 61** Loose jumping helps the horse to develop his natural jumping technique

Various modifications may be made to the individual fences to help to achieve a particular result; for example:

• Cross poles encourage a horse that is lazy with his forefeet to tuck them up high.
• An 'A' fence helps to straighten a horse that jumps crookedly, and is another way to encourage the horse to tuck up his forehand (see Fig 40).
• A pole placed on the ground exactly halfway between the elements of a double, encourages the horse to be more precise with his stride, and helps to make the stride between the fences bigger and rounder.
• Three trotting poles into the first jump encourage the horse to jump from trot, which helps to improve his activity and co-ordination into the first fence.

Loose jumping, like all the horse's other work, must be carried out in quiet but positive circumstances. He must not be chased down the lane, although initially it may be necessary for the trainer to encourage him from behind with the long whip. An assistant is necessary to catch him at the end of the exercise and to congratulate him if he has done well. For this work it is sensible to dress the horse in brushing boots on all four legs, and overreach boots on the forefeet. He can also be fitted with a stable head-collar to help when catching and leading him.

Loose jumping is therefore a useful exercise when introducing the young horse to jumping training; it is also a good way of providing variety in the trained horse's work, and can be used mid-season for the competition horse both to freshen up his attitude, and to help to re-establish good jumping technique which can, on occasions, deteriorate after a great deal of fast cross-country jumping. Further, horses that become tense and start to rush their fences, often benefit from occasional loose schooling down a jumping lane.

Ridden jumping training

The showjumping horse requires muscular strength and good wind; he does not require the endurance qualities of the cross-country or point-to-point horse – only in the top echelons of Grand Prix jumping and horse trials is the course as long as 800m. Nevertheless the horse that is over-weight is clearly at a disadvantage; he should be well covered, but without being fat.

Much of his suppleness and agility can be achieved by correct schooling on the flat; his strengthening, co-ordinating and technique-improving work will be contained in a well planned gymnastic training programme. This is best introduced by walking and trotting over poles on the ground; if trotting-pole work has been established on the lunge it should present no difficulties when ridden. It is very good for improving the horse's balance, agility and co-ordination, and is an appropriate way to combine training on the flat with jumping training. It also helps the rider to find a steady rhythm, and can influence the tempo and the length of the steps. Variety can be introduced by first walking, and eventually trotting over poles on the straight, on curves, on large circles (15 to 20m/18–22yd) or on the serpentine. Poles are best used in odd numbers – one, three or five; putting down poles in even numbers may tend to invite the horse to jump over them two at a time.

Initially the work can be done in walk, perhaps on a long rein to allow the horse to establish his own confidence and to approach the poles in a relaxed manner – he should take the rein, and stretch his head and neck forwards and down as he steps over each pole. To facilitate this it is, of course, important that the poles are placed an appropriate distance apart, about one metre for medium walk.

Work over ground poles should improve the trot. In all this work the horse should be obedient, relaxed and on the bit, without tension or resistance: if he attempts to rush the poles he must be circled away and worked on the circle until the desired relaxed attitude is re-established, when the exercise can be attempted again. Allowing the horse to rush the trotting poles will almost certainly result in him rushing his fences.

● **Fig 62** Raised trotting poles can be used to improve the activity of the pace

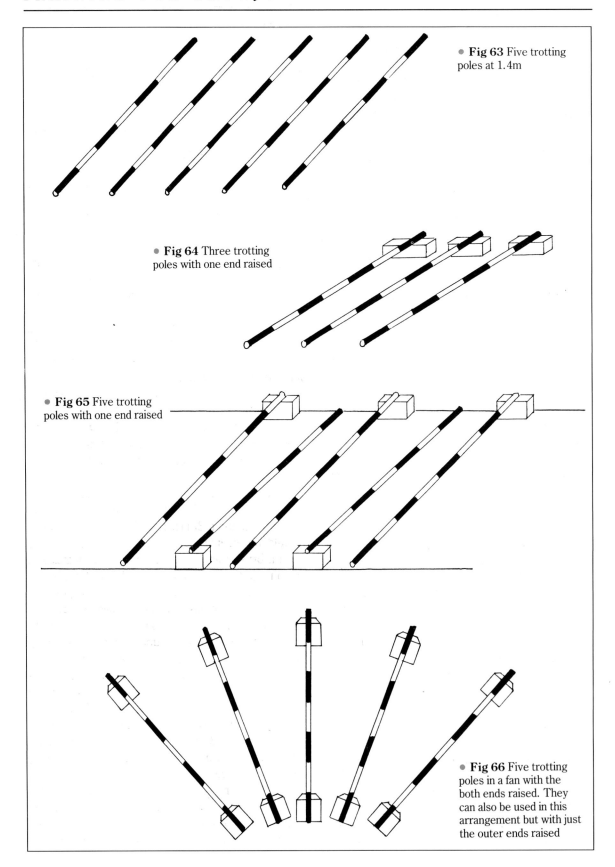

• **Fig 63** Five trotting poles at 1.4m

• **Fig 64** Three trotting poles with one end raised

• **Fig 65** Five trotting poles with one end raised

• **Fig 66** Five trotting poles in a fan with the both ends raised. They can also be used in this arrangement but with just the outer ends raised

Trotting pole exercises can be developed by raising the poles, first at one end only, then at both ends (see Fig 62); this encourages more engagement of the hind legs, and rounder, more elevated steps with greater spring. In a line of poles, alternate ends are raised to start with, to introduce the exercise progressively; later both ends are raised.

A selection of trotting pole exercises is shown in Figs 63–6.

GYMNASTIC JUMPING TRAINING

Varied work over poles on the ground leads logically to ridden gymnastic jumping. The successful trainer keeps in the front of his mind the importance of building confidence, good technique and strength, and gymnastic jumping helps to achieve all of these qualities. It helps to improve the technique of horse and rider because it encourages the striding and jumping to be precise; it also allows for remedial jumping exercises which can be put together to encourage good jumping and alleviate individual faults. It improves strength because it encourages the use of the correct jumping muscles in a controlled, repetitive way, thereby enhancing their development.

The facilities and equipment that are required are simple and usually easily accessible. A safe working area is a pre-requisite, either indoors or outside; and good going is most important, as repetitive work on either deep, hard or uneven going puts considerable strain on joints, tendons and ligaments. Also, it is best if this work can be conducted away from other distractions such as traffic, machinery or any other noise. The minimum amount of equipment that is required is about ten showjump poles not less than 3.6m in length, six cavaletti of some sort, and a selection of showjumping fillers – a small brush fence, a wall, etc. A dismounted assistant can be very helpful to assist in adjusting the equipment as and when required.

Gymnastic jumping instils confidence as the trainer/rider can be in full command of the approach to any jump, since the preceding elements can be placed in such a way that the horse arrives at the most advantageous point for take-off. This varies, of course, according to the type and height of the fence, but in general, in order to achieve a good bascule over the jump, the horse should take off in

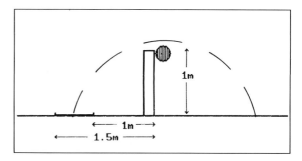

● **Fig 67** A good guide to the most advantageous take-off zone is that it should be between the height of the jump and the height and a half of the jump in front of the highest element of the jump

an area in front of the jump between the height and the height and a half of the obstacle (see Fig 67). This is clearly not so when tackling the puissance wall standing at over 2m, but for jumps up to 1.5m it is a good guide, and it means the trainer/rider can put a placing pole or fence at exactly the right distance in front of the jump so as to get the horse into the most advantageous position for take-off. Jumping from a good take-off zone gives the horse the confidence to canter into the jump on a good, strong canter stride, because he knows he will be exactly right in his striding and will not have to reach for the jump or put in a short, adjusting stride.

When the horse will trot over three or five trotting poles at about 1.3m to 1.4m apart, a jump can be added at about 3m to 3.5m from the last pole. It should be an inviting jump, perhaps cross-poles with a brush filling, and sufficiently substantial to encourage the horse to make a deliberate jumping effort. The height of the jump depends upon the stage of his training, and he should not be discouraged or over-faced. However, jumps that are too small frequently encourage careless jumping which is detrimental to the development of good technique. When the horse performs this exercise in a relaxed, confident way, a second jump can be added about 6.5m to 7m from the first – this distance enables him to take one good, balanced canter stride and reach the second jump in exactly the correct take-off zone. This second jump may be an upright fence, perhaps poles, but well filled and inviting. When a third jump is added the distance may need to be a little longer, 7m to 7.5m, as he will be well into his canter stride. However, the competent trainer/rider must study each individual

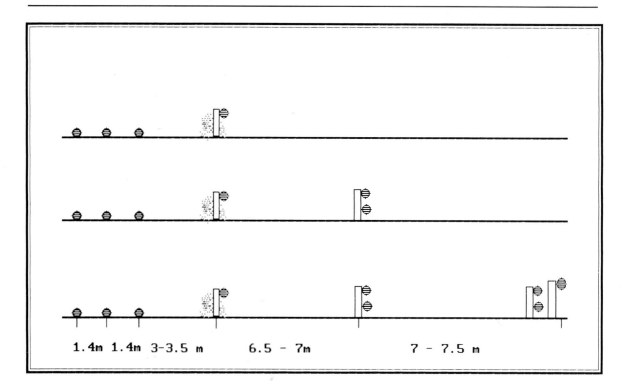

1.4m 1.4m 3-3.5 m   6.5 - 7m   7 - 7.5 m

• **Fig 68** A progressive gymnastic jumping course.

horse and adjust the distances to suit and encourage that particular horse.

The trotting poles and the first two jumps are designed to get the horse's attention and to develop impulsion, balance and co-ordination. The third fence can usefully be a little more of a test, perhaps an ascending oxer with the back pole 10cm higher than the front. It must be substantial, well filled and inviting to encourage bold jumping.

Any amount of variety can be put into this work by changing the nature of the jumps – the wall, various fillers, planks and even water trays can be included where appropriate. Also, the distances between the jumps can be varied, although they *must* always be true distances to encourage bold, accurate striding; but they can be set for a bounce about 3.5m (where no stride is taken), or for one or two strides (see Fig 68), and so on.

So far this gymnastic training has been carried out on straight lines only; the next stage is to introduce changes of direction. The imaginative trainer/ rider will introduce variety into all the horse's work, to create a challenge for his pupil and to prevent boredom. The following exercises are recommended in order to make progress in gymnastic training. The jumps are laid out as in Fig 69 and can be set up in an indoor school or an outside manège; a variety of fences can be used, which need only to be jumped in one direction. The approach is over three trotting-poles, set at about 1.30m with about 3m between the last pole and the first jump. Jump No 1 is a small inviting fence, a brushfiller at 0.7m with a pole over the top making the total height about 0.8m. Jump No 2 is an upright of poles at 0.8m; jump No 3 a small wall with a pole over the top at about 0.8m; jump No 4 is a parallel oxer at about 0.8m, with a 0.6m spread and a brush filler. The distance between jumps Nos 1 and 2, and 1 and 3, should be about 6m, as jump No 1 is approached from trot. The distance between No 2 and No 4, and No 3 and No 4, should be about 6.5m, as these will be approached from canter. Having warmed the horse up in his normal way, the exercises may be started as follows:

Exercise No 1: A good balanced working trot through the trotting poles and over fence No 1, three strides in canter going between the wings of fences Nos 2 and 3, and over fence No 4. This exercise can eventually be used to help the horse and rider to adjust the length of stride by halfhalting, and thus taking four canter steps between jumps 1 and 4.

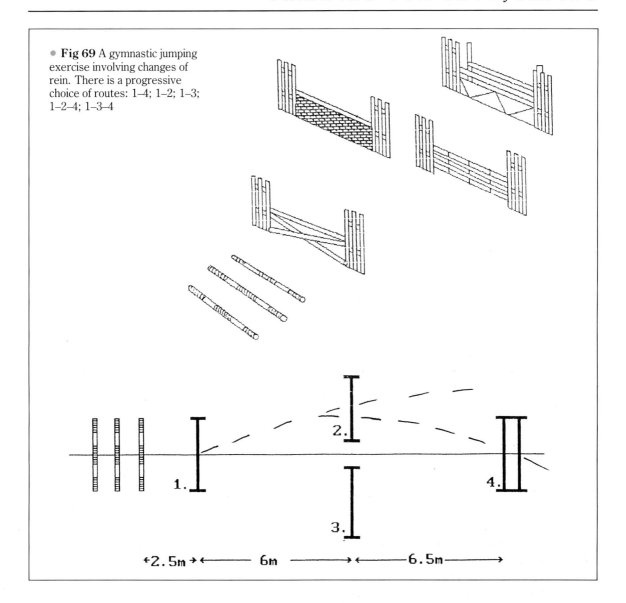

● **Fig 69** A gymnastic jumping exercise involving changes of rein. There is a progressive choice of routes: 1–4; 1–2; 1–3; 1–2–4; 1–3–4

Exercise No 2: Through the trotting poles and over jump No 1 looking towards jump No 2, one stride in canter and over No 2.

Exercise No 3: Through the trotting poles and over jump No 1 looking towards jump No 3, one stride in canter and over jump No 3.

Exercise No 4: Through the trotting poles and over jump No 1, looking towards jump No 2, one stride in canter and over jump No 2 looking towards jump No 4, one stride in canter and over jump No 4.

Exercise No 5: This is the same as exercise No 4 but made to the right.

The next gymnastic jumping exercise includes a series of 'doubles', frequent changes of direction, jumping some fences at an angle, and a variety of jumps; it requires the rider to ride the horse in a balanced fashion round a jumping course. The exercise consists of four jumps arranged as shown in Fig 70. Both upright and spread fences can be included, but they must be designed so that they can be jumped in both directions. For example No 1 may be an upright rustic pole and brush filler, No 2 a wall, No 3 planks, No 4 a square oxer. The distances between the various elements should be adjusted to suit the horse in training and the pace at which the exercise is to be ridden. If ridden from canter, indoors, on soft going the distance suitable for an average 16hh horse between fences would be between 7 and 7.5m.

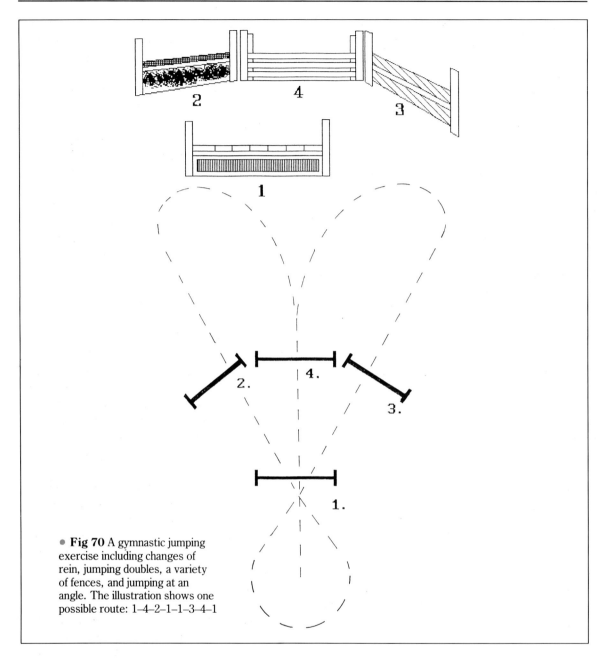

● **Fig 70** A gymnastic jumping exercise including changes of rein, jumping doubles, a variety of fences, and jumping at an angle. The illustration shows one possible route: 1–4–2–1–1–3–4–1

The exercise can be ridden from trot or canter. The main consideration is that, between the individual jumps, the horse remains calm, balanced and on the bit; if any of these qualities is lost, the rider has sufficient room to circle between the jumps until the situation is restored. A smooth, balanced track must be ridden, making the loops big enough so that each jump can be approached in good form, but not so big that time is wasted. Eventually it is a useful exercise for training both horse and rider to ride a timed jump-off in a confined space.

A variety of tracks can be ridden:

$$1-4-2-1-1-3-4-1$$
$$1-3-2-1-1-4-3-1$$
$$3-1-2-4-1$$

or any other combination that encourages balanced jumping.

An exercise to follow this one takes gymnastic training a stage further, and ensures variety – it includes trotting poles, a bounce between cross poles, and a spread fence set at a slight angle.

DIFFICULTIES ENCOUNTERED IN JUMPING TRAINING

There are a number of problems that unfortunately are encountered all too frequently by many who train jumpers. Often they are self-imposed, the fault of a trainer/rider who has made mistakes in basic training: for instance, asking the horse to jump fences for which he is not ready; going too fast in novice competitions; fitting equipment that compels or encourages the horse to go in a particular way before he is ready.

Rushing at fences

Horses sometimes rush their fences out of sheer enthusiasm and exuberance; however, whilst this enthusiasm should not be discouraged, control is soon lost if the horse is allowed to decide for himself the speed at which the course should be negotiated.

Otherwise, this problem may reflect the horse's natural reaction to fear or danger, which is to run away. He may be frightened because he has been hurt whilst jumping, or has been punished with the whip, spurs or rapping pole, in which case he may well resort to his natural instinct – flight. Clearly the cure for this problem is that his confidence must be restored.

The desired result may be achieved by circling him, in trot, in front of the fence until he has forgotten about jumping and is quiet and relaxed. He is then trotted into the jump, and on landing is encouraged to return quietly to a trot circle. The trainer must be in no hurry to jump again, and should return to the trot circle in front of the jump until the required degree of relaxation has been re-established.

Another ploy which is often successful is to walk the horse up to a small inviting fence and halt three or four metres from the fence. The reins are then dropped, and the horse is allowed to stand for a minute or two whilst the rider talks to him and pats him on the neck. It also helps if the trainer, dismounted, stands directly in front of him, between the horse and the jump, and close to his head where he, too, can talk to him and pat him on the neck in order to take his mind off jumping. The horse must stand straight, calm and relaxed. The reins are then taken up quietly and he is asked to walk forward for a step or two, and trot over the fence.

Rushing the jump is often brought about by a nervous or unskilled rider. If the rider causes the horse discomfort in any phase of the jump – the approach, take-off, flight or landing – the association may well cause him to rush his fences. This discomfort may be caused because the rider loses his balance or is left behind, by uneven or rough rein contact, excessive use of the legs and seat, or any other form of over-riding. A quiet, competent rider produces a quiet, confident horse; a nervous, over-active rider produces an anxious one.

The horse that rushes may be doing so because jumping actually hurts him in some way. Expert veterinary examination, or an equine chiropractor, may be able to help – the skills of this profession are becoming widely acknowledged.

Refusing and running out

Horses that develop either or both of these resistances are potentially unreliable as competition horses. Both types of disobedience can be overcome, often permanently, but the horse has a very good memory and once he has learned to refuse or run out it may always remain at the back of his mind as a possible option to jumping. That is why the trainer/rider should be very careful that the horse is never put in a situation in training where he is tempted to refuse or run out. And it is just as important that the rider himself is sufficiently skilled, effective and determined in schooling the horse over fences and between them. The trainer and rider must ensure that the horse is never overfaced, taking the trouble to construct safe, inviting fences, and never over-jumping the horse so that he becomes stale or tired.

To correct a horse that has developed, or is developing, either of these resistances, careful preparation is required and any situation that may encourage him to refuse or run out should be avoided. The following points might advantageously be noted:

1 The rider must be competent and confident: the disobedient or nervous horse quickly recognises the absence of either of these qualities in the rider.

2 Any practice jump must be carefully prepared: first, it should be an appropriate height, and certainly not so high that the horse is tempted to try to avoid it in some way. A narrow jump

such as a stile is uninviting; much more encouraging is a wide fence, built from at least 3.5m (4yd) rustic poles, with stout wings and well filled with brush. A clear ground-line helps to make the jump inviting; too much daylight in the bottom of the fence tends to be off-putting. The importance of building substantial wings cannot be over-stressed: they must be considerably higher than, and wide enough to show clearly the part of the fence that is to be jumped. They must make the alternative – running out – seem unattractive.

3   Difficult, 'trappy' fences should be avoided. These might include corner-jumps, or jumps into the dark, or out of the dark into bright light – in fact anything that is off-putting for the horse. Bright, unusual colours, shapes and patterns may discourage a horse that is anyway lacking in confidence, and should be avoided whilst the problems of refusing or running out are being corrected.

4   Good going is important. If the horse is reluctant to jump anyway, a deep boggy take-off area will only make him even more inclined to refuse, as will a hard take-off area that he may find is jarring, or gives poor footing.

5   The approach to the jump should be straight, that is at right-angles to the face of the jump. The ability to jump at an angle must be developed in the competition horse, but it is an invitation to run out for the disobedient horse.

6   The jump must be approached at the appropriate speed and with the right amount of impulsion. Galloping into a jump, on the forehand and too fast, encourages the horse to run out or refuse. Over-checking into a jump without maintaining the forward impulse also invites a refusal.

7   Whilst the horse must be ridden forwards with energy and determination, over-use of the whip and spur will only make him associate jumping with painful, unpleasant experiences and may compound the problem. The whip, when used as a punishment, must be a short, sharp reprimand given so it coincides exactly with the disobedience – the horse must associate the sting of the whip with the disobedient act, and only then will he be discouraged from doing it again. Using the whip minutes after the disobedience is of no use whatsoever.

Hitting the jumps with the fore or hind feet

One of the qualities of a good showjumping horse is his dislike for hitting jumps with his feet, legs or knees. Some horses have this natural sense of self-preservation, others are careless and do not seem to mind hitting the fence. Sometimes this is due to sheer laziness on the horse's part, because he discovers how much easier it is to knock down the top pole than to jump 5cm higher. This fault can sometimes be rectified by ensuring that he is awake and active when coming into the jump. It takes skilled riding by a rider to keep the horse between the leg and hand, and who knows when a touch with the whip is required to keep the horse's attention.

Other horses that knock off a top pole are confident, bold jumpers who find their work easy and are consequently careless. These are less easy to correct, as their bold approach must not be discouraged.

In both cases, work that improves the jumping technique is required. The horse must learn to respect the fence and know that it hurts if he hits it. To this end, lightweight jumping poles made from plastic or lightweight wood should be avoided – the horse soon learns when the poles or wings are light and unstable and can be kicked over without any difficulty. The top pole at least must be hard and heavy enough for the horse to know that it will hurt if he hits it.

Showjumping course builders and designers are constantly trying to provide variety in the fences that they use. Thus a new type of filler or wing may distract the inexperienced horse from the job in hand, resulting in faults being incurred. With this in mind the trainer/rider should school the competition horse over the widest possible variety of show jumps. A selection of the most common types that may be found in novice competitions is shown in Figs 55–60.

Horses in training often become too complacent if they are schooled regularly over the same fences, so it is important to provide variety in both the location and the jump material that is used. Fig 73 shows the horse being schooled over an 'A' fence; this was recommended for loose jumping (see p82) and is useful in ridden work to encourage the horse to jump straight and to tuck up the forehand. A fence incorporating cross-poles in the front element also encourages the horse to fold up

• **Fig 71** Jumping in good style over a parallel oxer

• **Fig 72** A pole placed diagonally across the top of the oxer encourages him to look at the schooling fence

● **Fig 73** Two poles placed as an 'A' on an upright fence will encourage extra care with the forefeet

his forelegs and pick up his feet to avoid hitting the poles.

Fig 72 shows the horse being schooled over a parallel oxer with a pole rested diagonally across the top of the jump. This merely serves as a safe way to encourage the horse to look at the jump and to pay attention to what he is doing.

Finally, as in all equestrian disciplines, each horse must be trained according to his own requirements and temperament. The amount and type of work he will take can only be assessed by the skill and experience of the trainer/rider. The heavier types of horse, the Irish Draught and heavy continental horses for instance, may require and will probably be able to stand a more repetitive and harder working programme than the Thoroughbred who is temperamentally and physically less suited to this type of work. But only the experienced trainer can tell.

As a general rule, jumping training is best done on a 'little and often' basis. Over-jumping a horse in training, either by the time spent jumping, the frequency of the jumping sessions, or the height and spread of the training obstacles, can easily make a good jumping horse stale. Fast work is seldom included in jumping training. Whilst some schooling over fences at the maximum height required in the competition is included in the programme, most training jumps are set at a height that does not require competition effort on the part of the horse.

Figs 74–81 show a variety of showjumping styles adopted by some riders and horses.

Fig 74 Tidy tucking up of the forelegs and good use of the head and neck

Fig 75 A neat and tidy technique from both horse and rider

Fig 76 A good jump over an ascending oxer

• **Fig 77** Failing to fold up the forelegs requires the horse
to jump higher than really necessary

• **Fig 78** This rider's poor technique has caused the horse
to jump untidily and hollow

• **Fig 79** An example of weak jumping technique, hollow and with all legs dangling

• **Fig 80** Bad technique from both horse and rider. The horse appears to have been thrown over the jump head-first

• **Fig 81** Well tucked-up forefeet

SEVEN

TRAINING FOR CROSS-COUNTRY JUMPING

● **Fig 82** Little Badminton: an upright cross-country fence between 3ft 9in and 3ft 11in (1.14m to 1.19m) high

Much of the training that is done with the show-jumping horse will benefit the cross-country horse. The agility, confidence, balance and co-ordination required are common to both horses; the courage and technique required are rather different. The showjumping horse must be brave enough to attempt big, unnatural obstacles in a confined space. Most of the obstacles that he is asked to jump he will have seen before, and he knows that the take-off and landing areas are constant and safe. The cross-country horse is not asked to jump fences as high as those found in the showjumping ring, but he must have the courage to jump un-known fences from a gallop, much faster than the pace asked of the showjumper. The going on which he is required to work may vary from day to day and even several times within one cross-country course. The type of courage required from these two horses is therefore rather different. The showjumping horse is seldom asked to jump a track longer than 800 metres, and faster than at 400 metres per minute, but the cross-country horse may have to jump a track as long as 6,200 metres at 570 metres per minute with up to thirty obstacles. The degree and type of physical fitness demanded of these two horses is therefore quite different.

Cross-country fences

These are intended to look as natural as possible, and fall into a number of types:

1 **Upright fences.** These include a five-bar gate, a post-and-rail fence or a stone wall for instance. See Figs 82, 91.

2 **Banks.** A solid mound which may or may not incorporate a fence. It is the type of bank that divides fields in some areas. See Fig 83.

3 **Open ditches.** A ditch in front of a fence making it into a spread. See Fig 84.

4 **Drop fences.** Any fence where the landing is lower than the take-off. See Figs 85, 90.

5 **Coffins.** A combination of jumps that involves one or more ditches. See Fig 86.

6 **Steps.** Jumps where the horse jumps up or down a series of steps. See Fig 87.

7 **Spread fences.** These are fences with breadth as well as height and include tables, log piles and parallel oxers of stout timber. See Figs 88, 92.

8 **Water jumps.** Any type of jump where the horse is required to jump into or out of water, or both. See Fig 89.

9 **The fly fence or steeplechase fence.** This fence is made from brush and gorse usually with a guard rail. It may include a ditch on the take-off or the landing side. It is the type of fence found in point-to-point or National Hunt racing. See Fig 93.

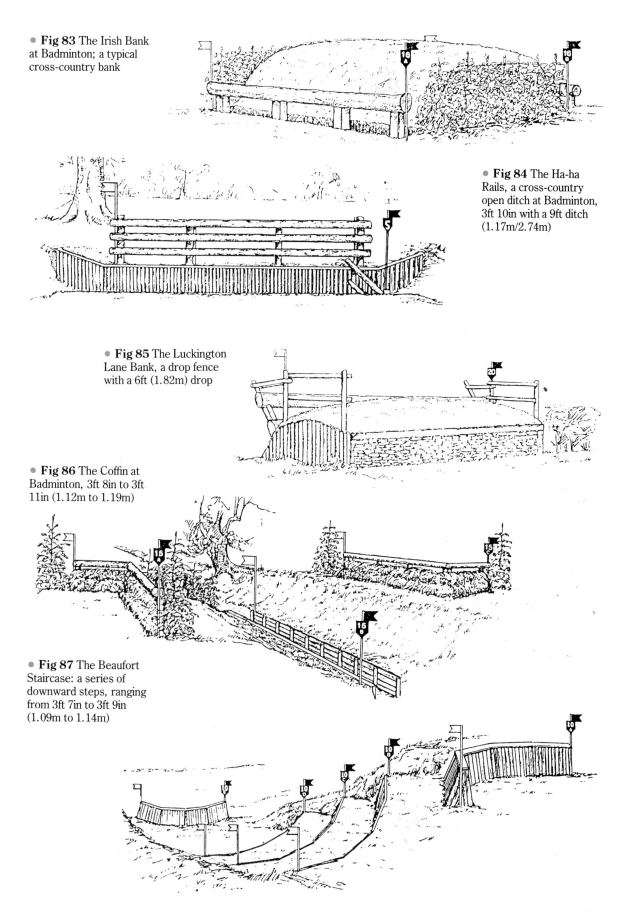

- **Fig 83** The Irish Bank at Badminton; a typical cross-country bank

- **Fig 84** The Ha-ha Rails, a cross-country open ditch at Badminton, 3ft 10in with a 9ft ditch (1.17m/2.74m)

- **Fig 85** The Luckington Lane Bank, a drop fence with a 6ft (1.82m) drop

- **Fig 86** The Coffin at Badminton, 3ft 8in to 3ft 11in (1.12m to 1.19m)

- **Fig 87** The Beaufort Staircase: a series of downward steps, ranging from 3ft 7in to 3ft 9in (1.09m to 1.14m)

• **Fig 88** A novel spread fence at Badminton

• **Fig 89** Jumps into water are usually best taken from trot
or a shortened canter

• **Fig 90** Solid fences encourage bold jumping; this example was seen at Gatcombe Park

• **Fig 91** A simple-looking obstacle which required a great deal of care as it was approached across a narrow wooden bridge over a ditch

• **Fig 92** Jumping big timber at Gatcombe Park

● **Fig 93** On the steeplechase course at Badminton

On a cross-country course, the course builder has many opportunities to test the skill and courage of both horse and rider. A comparatively small fence can be made very difficult by the position in which it is placed.

Training facilities

Finding facilities for cross-country training is a task that confronts every trainer and rider. Continual schooling over the same jumps is of limited value, as variety is the essence of cross-country competition. The good cross-country horse must have sufficiently wide experience to take on any fence whether he has seen it before or not. Hunting in good country can be invaluable. It teaches the horse to go in company with others and introduces him to strange sights and sounds that will stand him in good stead under competition conditions. Added to this, it provides the opportunity to gallop on land, and jump a wide variety of fences that would otherwise be unavailable. The minus side of hunting is the poor day, in limited country, where horse and rider stand around in the cold and wet for long periods. This does nothing for the preparation of a competition horse. Drag-hunting is a useful substitute. It provides a series of prepared fences over a measured distance, which makes the organisation and administration of the training session very much easier.

Cross-country training must include schooling over the various types of fence described.

Some fences can, and should, be jumped from gallop: steeplechase fences, bullfinches, stone walls and post-and-rail fences, when set on open land, come into this category. Fences that are built to school over in gallop must be solid and impressive to ensure that the horse makes a true effort to jump them. Galloping into flimsy fences, ie those made of light material with a lot of daylight showing, can be dangerous if the horse feels that he can gallop through them.

Other fences, particularly those with a restricted approach, may have to be taken from trot. Sufficient schooling in jumping from trot must be done to ensure that the horse will come back to trot when told to do so.

The water obstacle

Training for jumping water obstacles sometimes presents problems where facilities are difficult to find. But every opportunity should be taken to ride the horse in and out of water, even if it only consists of walking through every available puddle. No opportunity should be missed to ride in and out of a stream or suitable river. Where possible, it is useful to put a cavaletti or showjump on the bank of a stream or in the water to school over. Horses that are reluctant to go into water should be given a lead by a confident horse, or even led by the trainer on foot. In circumstances where difficulties are encountered, once he is in the water he should not be allowed straight out, but should be hacked around getting used to the feel of it, and gaining confidence that the bottom is safe to stand on. Training at a water obstacle should, like all training, be progressive. He should first be asked to walk in quietly, feeling his way, but should not be allowed to step back. When he will walk in and out, he should be trotted in and out, and later jumped in from trot over a low cavaletti, which can, over a period of time, be increased to a small jump.

● **Fig 94** Encourage your horse to relax in water

● **Fig 95** A typical water complex in a novice horse trial

● **Fig 96** (above) Bold jumping of a corner fence
● **Fig 97** (right) A deep drop fence
● **Fig 98** (opposite) Lucinda Green negotiating the steps at Gatcombe Park

The corner fence

A corner fence is often set on a cross-country course, usually as part of a complex with one or more options, the corner being the most difficult option (see Fig 96). To reduce the spread it is tempting to jump as close to the flag as possible, but this is inviting a run-out; yet the further away from the flag one gets, the greater the spread. The safest way to negotiate it is at right angles to the line that bisects the corner, and far enough in from the flag to be safe. Attempting to jump the front element at too much of an angle is to risk running out. It is a useful jump to be able to take well and with confidence, as it may save precious seconds.

A ditch presents problems for some horses, in which case no opportunity should be missed to school over ditches from walk, trot or canter.

LIBRARY
BISHOP BURTON COLLEGE
BEVERLEY HU17 8QG

LUNGEING AND LONG-REINING

Dismounted training consists mainly of lungeing and long-reining, and is a most interesting and important part of the preparation of a competition horse.

THE VALUE OF LUNGEING

Lungeing can be used effectively at all stages of the horse's training in a number of situations:

1 The training of a young horse is started on the lunge. When he can be led safely from both sides, work on the lunge can be started. This, under normal circumstances, will be when he is three years old. If started earlier than this, there is a possibility that undue strain may be put on joints and tendons which are not yet fully mature. Lungeing the young horse in preparation for backing teaches him manners, it trains him to respond to the trainer's/rider's words of command, develops balance, agility, suppleness and co-ordination, and begins the strengthening of the muscles that are to support both the horse and rider when he is backed. It also provides the opportunity to fit the saddle and bridle, and to teach the horse to accept these before the rider is introduced. Work on the lunge is also the first opportunity for the trainer to start the important work of establishing the basic paces.

2 It sometimes occurs that the fit horse, for some reason, cannot be ridden on a particular day, but must be kept on full rations. It is possible to work a horse on the lunge sufficiently to be able to do this (see page 113).

3 As the horse's training progresses there are aspects of his work that may be best introduced on the lunge. Jumping is one of these, and teaching the horse to lengthen the steps in trot is often more easily started on the lunge than when ridden.

4 Some horses respond well to being lunged before ridden work is started. This is particularly useful before a competition where all the showground distractions – flags flying, the noise of loud-speakers, the presence of other horses and so on – may cause tension and excitement in an inexperienced horse, and in some experienced ones, too. A quiet period on the lunge often settles the horse and makes the rider's task easier once he is mounted.

5 Training the rider on the lunge is a technique that should be mastered by all competition trainers – it is useful for beginner riders, and equally useful for correcting and enhancing the seat and understanding of competent riders as well. Most competition riders, no matter how successful, can benefit from a lesson on the lunge from time to time. (See page 131–2.)

Where to lunge: surroundings and going

Selecting an area on which to lunge is the first important consideration: ideally it will be away from other distractions in a secluded situation; it must be flat, of good going, and large enough to make at least a 20m circle and if possible some straight lines as well. If this work has to be done in a field it is best, at first, to use a corner where two fences converge and give some guidance. A small paddock is better than the corner of, say, a 5-hectare field.

Grass may be satisfactory going, but it can be slippery when it is wet or when the ground is dry and hard. Furthermore, the ring made by lungeing a horse on soft grass may last many months. Thus a sand, wood-chip or other composite surface is best, provided that it is not too deep.

Specially designed lungeing arenas are sometimes built, some with roofs and some open, consisting of a sand floor and a circular fence that enables the trainer to lunge the horse on a 20m circle or smaller. They are convenient and easy to use; but lungeing should not be thought of simply as an exercise where the horse runs round the trainer in a circle because he has no alternative, rather like the liberty horse in the circus. Lungeing must be 'dismounted riding', where the trainer is in full command with the horse between the whip and lunge-rein; he must be able to move the circle as he wishes, change from a circle to a square, perhaps make some straight lines. This he is unable to do in a lungeing arena, and the risk of the horse becoming utterly bored working in these surroundings should not be overlooked. An arena is, however, a useful place in which to introduce the young horse to work on the lunge.

LUNGEING EQUIPMENT

To lunge efficiently the correct equipment is required; ad-hoc equipment is not advisable as it may have undesirable side-effects. The items of tack and clothing which are necessary are described below, and as in all such areas, certain designs and materials are more effective than others.

The lungeing cavesson

A lungeing cavesson made from either leather or nylon (see Fig 99) is best; neither a stable head-collar nor a bridle is a suitable substitute. It is used at first on its own, and later, when the bit is required, in conjunction with a snaffle bridle from which the noseband and browband have been removed. It should be lightweight – those that are fitted with a browband, or double throat-lashes, or a central support for the noseband, become heavy and cumbersome. It must have sufficient adjustment to be a snug fit without being too tight. A loose lungeing cavesson is ineffective, and runs the risk of slipping so that the outside cheekpiece comes into contact with the horse's outside eye,

● **Fig 99** The lungeing cavesson and snaffle bridle correctly fitted

which is clearly undesirable. The noseband should be adjusted until it fits closely around the nose, about 3cm (1¼in) below the facial crest; the throat-lash should be fitted a little closer than a bridle throat-lash.

There are normally three rings on the noseband of a lungeing cavesson: the lunge rein is fitted to the centre ring, and those on either side are best used for fitting the side-reins in the initial stages before they are fitted to the bit. They are also useful for starting work on the long-reins. Occasionally the lungeing cavesson is fitted as a 'Wels' cavesson, that comes below the bit, rather like a drop noseband. This can be useful when problems can be foreseen on the lunge, perhaps because in the past the horse has been allowed to be disobedient, or has been badly trained in some other way. A young stallion who has grown to 16hh at three years old and has not been handled, may respond well to lungeing in the 'Wels' cavesson. It is, however, very severe and should only be used with care and by an experienced trainer.

• **Fig 100** Working well on the lunge

Horses are sometimes lunged from a snaffle bridle, when the lunge-rein is clipped to the outside ring of the bit, passed over the poll and threaded through the inside ring of the bit and thence to the trainer's hand. This provides strong control, but it does make the bit into a severe gag, and the action of the bit on the corners of the mouth is very sharp.

The lunge-rein

This can be made from webbing, lampwick or nylon. Some trainers prefer a ploughline or rope, but the feel in the hand with a rope is nothing like the feel of a riding rein – and the aim of lungeing is, after all, to be 'dismounted riding'. A convenient length for this rein would be about 7–8m (7½–8½yd), as it would then allow work on a good-sized circle, yet not be so long that it becomes cumbersome to use. A strong spring-clip on a swivel is fitted to one end (a leather end with a swivel, buckle and spring-clip is unnecessary and cumbersome), and there would be a loop of about 20cm (8in) on the other end. The trainer puts three fingers only through this loop so

that he can keep hold of the rein in an emergency. The rein is held between the third finger and the little finger, as one would hold the snaffle rein when riding (see Figs 101–2); in this way a similar feel in the hand can be achieved with the lunge rein as would be felt with the snaffle rein when riding.

There are other acceptable methods of holding the lunge-rein: some trainers pass the rein over the top of the index finger to the cavesson (Fig 101); others hold the rein in the hand folded into a 'figure of eight' (Fig 102). It is less easy to lengthen and shorten the rein with this technique, but some feel that the hand is less likely to be trapped should the horse pull violently. The method that is adopted must suit the individual trainer – but whichever is used, he must have good control of the rein, and be able to lengthen and shorten it as required. He must also be able to maintain a sure, steady contact through the rein and cavesson to the horse.

The lungeing whip

A lungeing whip is required with a lash long enough to reach the horse when he is working on a circle of

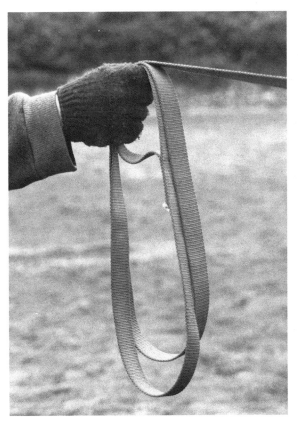 

• **Figs 101–2** Two ways of holding the lunge rein

about 16m (17yd) diameter. It should not be too heavy (as some are). The whip is held in the right hand as the horse works to the left, and in the left hand as he works to the right. It is used in conjunction with the voice aids and is directed towards the hocks or hind quarter to encourage the horse forwards, and towards the shoulder to encourage him to stay out on the circle. It should *not* be cracked as this only causes alarm, and it is undesirable that the horse should jump forward when he hears a crack. As the horse works on the circle, the lash of the whip should be allowed to trail behind the trainer; when its influence is required it can then be 'thrown' towards the horse – it is very difficult to use the lash of the whip if it is allowed to hang in a pile under the whip-handle. When two hands are required to hold the lunge rein, perhaps in an emergency, the whip can be held under one arm with the lash to the rear. The usual method is to hold the rein in one hand with the loops neatly folded and the whip in the other; though some trainers prefer to hold the rein in one hand and the loops and the whip in the other. Either method is acceptable provided that it is efficient, functional and safe.

Side-reins

Side-reins are an important part of lungeing equipment (see Fig 103). They are fitted to keep the horse straight, or at least to discourage him from bending his neck too much to the left or to the right. When used in training the young horse they are a useful way to encourage him to seek a contact with the bit. When training the rider on the lunge, or when lungeing the trained horse, they enable the trainer to work the horse 'on the bit'.

Various types are available, but the plain leather variety is thought to be the best. Some are fitted with elastic inserts, but these may discourage the horse from accepting the bit steadily. Others are fitted with a rubber ring in each rein to provide some elasticity; however, these rings are quite heavy and tend to bounce up and down as the horse trots, which is distracting and also interrupts the contact of the bit on the horse's mouth. The rein is fitted to the bit-ring, and to the girth or the saddle at its other end. The height of the rein at the saddle

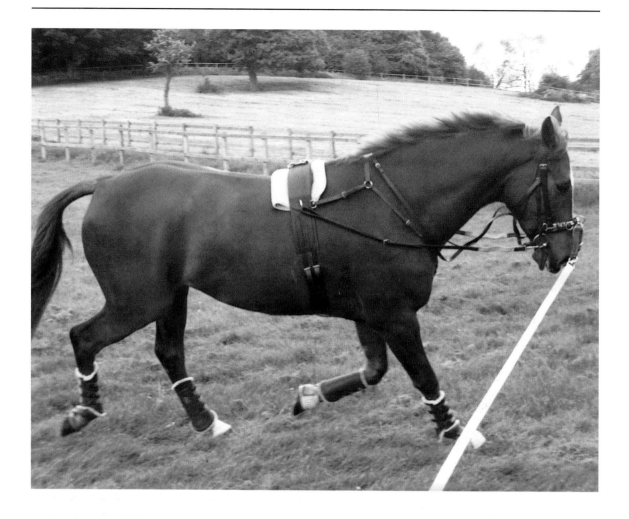

● **Fig 103** The side-reigns used on the lunge

end is important: at first, with the young horse, it will be adjusted so that the rein is about parallel to the ground, as this will encourage him to stretch forward to seek the bit. Later, as the work progresses, the saddle-end of the side-rein can be raised so that it approaches the position in which the rider's hands would be if the horse were being ridden.

The side-reins should be adjusted so that they are of equal length. It is fairly common practice to fit the inside rein a hole or two shorter than the outside rein, but the result of this is to bend the neck only; in consequence the outside shoulder often 'falls out' and the horse is crooked on the circle.

The side-reins should also be adjusted in length to suit the stage of training for any particular horse. For the young horse who is only just being introduced to working with a contact on the bit they will

be long, with just the weight of the rein resting on his mouth. As he progresses and works in a rounder outline the side-reins are made shorter. Eventually, when he is performing perhaps dismounted piaffe as a part of his work, they will be short enough for him to work in a high degree of collection. They are only ever fitted when they are required to have an effect on the work that the horse is doing: they are taken off as soon as that particular work is completed.

Protective boots

The horse that is being lunged is quite likely to injure himself by brushing – one foot striking into the opposite leg – or by over-reaching. The simple precaution of fitting brushing boots or exercise bandages to all four legs, and overreach boots to the forelegs, will provide a degree of protection; Yorkshire boots should be sufficient to protect the fetlock joints of the hind legs.

Saddle or roller

Either a saddle or a lungeing roller is required to which the side-reins can be fitted. If a saddle is used, the stirrups and leathers should be either removed or secured as shown in Fig 104. A lungeing roller should be fitted with a breast girth to prevent it slipping back and putting unintended weight on the side-reins.

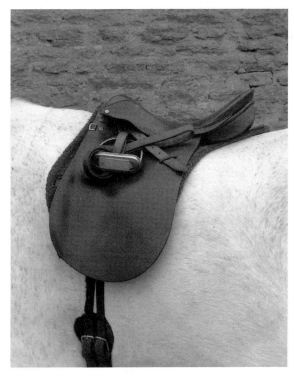

● **Fig 104** The stirrups safely secured for lungeing

Gloves

Untrained or poorly trained horses, or those that are just high-spirited, can become quite strong on the lunge, putting considerable strain on the trainer's hands. As in all dismounted training with the horse, a pair of gloves is an essential item in the trainer's equipment.

LUNGEING TECHNIQUE

The technique and attitude of the trainer are an essential part of effective lungeing. Even though the handling of lungeing equipment may *look* simple, it is not, and it can be difficult, if not dangerous, when the handling of the rein and the whip is not efficient. The trainer must stand in a relaxed and balanced way ready to move in any direction to keep the horse going forward and between the whip and hand. At first it may be necessary for the trainer to walk a circle, keeping just behind the horse's shoulder to ensure that he continues to go forward. For the trainer to stand even a little in front of the horse is an invitation for him to turn in and halt, or even change the rein. Once the horse understands what he is required to do on the lunge, the trainer should attempt to stand still in the centre of the circle, pivoting on his left foot as the horse works to the left, and on his right foot as the horse works to the right. This principle leads to tidy work and the horse learning to make a circle that is geometrically correct. The trainer must, however, be prepared to move quickly should circumstances demand; he will have decided which method of holding the lunge rein suits him best, but he must be able to maintain an elastic contact through the rein to the horse. A soft bend in the trainer's elbow and a supple shoulder allows this elastic contact to be maintained, and enables the trainer to vary the size of the circles by half a metre or so without adjusting the length of the rein. The lunge rein should be kept straight – allowing it to sag or trail on the ground may be dangerous, and a slack rein means that the horse is no longer between the whip and hand. Twists in the rein should also be avoided, as they spoil the feel in the hand; and it is important that the trainer is able to let the rein out longer and take it up shorter as needed. This requires the rein to be in tidy loops. Thus when a change of rein is made, the trainer puts the rein into his new rein-hand and takes up the loops in that hand as he walks up to the horse; the loops will then be ready for tidy work on the new rein.

Words of command

The number of words of command used should be kept to a minimum: 'walk on', 'walk', 'trot', 'canter' and 'woah' should be sufficient, and in fact it is the tone of the trainer's voice that achieves the required result. For an upward transition, where an increase in activity is required, a sharp word of command is best – 'terr-ot', for instance. For a downward transition, a long-drawn-out word of command is more successful: '. . .and, waaalk' is usually effective. The horse soon learns to understand these words of command provided they are used consistently and accompanied by the appropriate whip- and rein-aids. Should the horse fail to respond to a word of command for an upward transition, it should be repeated and accompanied by a touch of the whip on the hind quarter. If he fails to respond to a word of command for a downward transition, the word should be repeated and accompanied by short, sharp tugs on the rein to regain his attention.

Tit-bits should be avoided as a reward, and particularly when lungeing as they tend to encourage the horse to turn in when he halts. This is an irritating fault which seems to come very easily to some horses, and is difficult to cure. When the horse is told to halt he must stand straight, on the circle, until he is instructed otherwise.

Size of circle

The size of the circle on which the horse is lunged is important. The general principle must be that it should not be so small that it puts strain on the horse, damaging joints or tendons; nor should it be so large that the trainer is unable to exercise full control. When preparing a young horse for backing, the circle must be not less than 16m (17yd) diameter to start with: this should avoid muscle strain and the possibility of damaging immature soft bones. The advanced horse, working in collection, may be lunged on a circle as small as 10 metres (11yd).

The diameter of the circle must therefore be adjusted to suit the size of the horse, his natural balance, agility and co-ordination, and his standard of training.

LUNGEING THE YOUNG HORSE

If the young horse has been led in hand from both sides in walk and trot and is obedient to the voice aids, lungeing should come easily to him at three years old. By this time he will probably be used to wearing a rug and roller, so fitting the lungeing roller should present no difficulties. If he has been well handled he should be confident, and his good manners should be well on the way to being established.

There are several reasons in favour of lungeing the young horse prior to backing:

1 | To improve fitness, build muscle and encourage suppleness, balance, co-ordination and agility.

2 | To establish the basic paces with a good rhythm, steady tempo, and cadence before the rider is introduced.

3 | To establish submission and obedience to the voice aids.

4 | To introduce the horse to working with a saddle and a secure girth, a bit and bridle, and protective boots. It is as well to have him accepting this equipment before backing is attempted.

For his first lungeing lesson the horse will be fitted with the lungeing cavesson, lunge-rein, and protective boots or bandages on all four feet. For this lesson it is best to have an assistant who will lead the horse by a short rein attached to the centre ring on the cavesson (see Fig 105). The trainer will stand in the centre of a 16m (17yd) circle with the horse on the lunge-rein, while the assistant leads the horse on the circle from the inside, ensuring that he walks forward on the trainer's word of command and halts on the word of command. The assistant should aim to walk at the horse's shoulder so that there is no question of him pulling the horse forwards. If the pupil responds well to the trainer's commands he can be rewarded by a pat on the neck from the assistant. If he fails to respond, the assistant can either give him a tap with a short whip to encourage him forwards, or a feel on the rein to ask him to halt. The principle of 'the association of ideas' is most important in horse training: a willing, obedient response on the part of the horse should be immediately rewarded by a pat on the neck and some encouraging words. A deliberately disobedient resistance must be immediately accompanied by a reprimand. The use of the whip must never be thought of as a punishment, but nevertheless a short, sharp slap on the flank lets the horse know that his resistant act is not allowed.

Once the horse will walk, trot and halt on both reins to the trainer's command, the assistant is no longer necessary; first he should disconnect his lead-rein and just walk beside the horse, and eventually leave him altogether by moving down the rein towards the trainer. However, he (the assistant) should be available for the next few lungeing sessions in case the training should regress.

As far as possible the work should be conducted equally on both reins. If a horse is particularly

difficult on one rein, perhaps through stiffness, it is unreasonable to work him excessively on that rein in order to make him 'softer' in that direction. The work should be done predominantly on his easier rein, and as progress is made on that rein the direction can be changed to his more difficult side. Then before he becomes stiff or the work begins to deteriorate, he should be changed back to the easier rein. The object must be eventually to have him working equally well on both reins; though it may be that 100 per cent equality will never be achieved.

Work on the lunge is physically quite demanding, and should only be expected of the horse for a short period of time. Initially it is enough for the young horse to work 5 to 10 minutes, perhaps to a maximum of 15 minutes split up into short periods of 2 or 3 minutes. Quite apart from the physical damage that may be done, there is also the risk of boredom, which may result in the horse losing enthusiasm for his work.

● **Fig 105** For the initial lunge lessons it is helpful to have an assistant to lead the horse

Throughout this work the circle must be kept as large as possible, commensurate with the trainer being able to remain in control.

As progress is made on the lunge, the bit can be introduced. In order to do this tidily the browband and noseband should be removed from a snaffle bridle before it is fitted, together with the lungeing cavesson (see Fig 99).

The next stage is to fit the lungeing roller or a saddle; if the horse has worn a rug and roller this should not present any difficulty. It is usually best to put it on in an indoor school or small paddock in case he protests. The saddle or lungeing roller must always be fitted with a breast girth to ensure that they cannot slip back, and this should be secured before the girth is done up.

When the horse accepts the saddle and bridle and will lunge on both reins in walk and trot, the side-reins can be introduced. These are fitted loosely at first so that only the weight of the rein is on the horse's mouth; they should be of equal length and parallel to the ground. When he accepts the side-reins he is probably ready for backing – although once this is done, there is no need for his training on the lunge to finish.

The next progressive stage is to lunge him over a pole on the ground. If he has been led over a pole from time to time in his early handling, this should not present a problem. The side-reins are disconnected and a rustic pole is put on the ground in a convenient place. The horse is lunged, on his easier rein, so that the circle just passes the end of the pole. When the trot circle is established the trainer takes a step or two towards the end of the pole so that it crosses the circle and the horse can trot over it. When he does this confidently on both reins, two more poles can be added in a fan shape, making three in all, at 1.20–1.40m (4–5ft) apart at the centres. Two poles are not recommended, as they tend not to encourage good trot steps and the horse may be tempted to jump them both together. However, with more than two these distances *do* encourage good trot steps for the average horse, although to achieve the best results they must be adjusted to suit the individual horse. This work is best done in trot, though in some circumstances it may be introduced in walk. The advantage of having the poles arranged in a fan, instead of a straight line, is that the trainer can adjust the length of the steps the horse takes by making the circle either larger or smaller. If any difficulty is encountered at the start of this exercise the assistant should be re-called to lead the horse through the poles.

CONTINUATION TRAINING ON THE LUNGE

As the horse's training progresses, it is often an advantage to work on the lunge with exercises that must eventually be ridden – it is clearly an advantage to introduce him to some work unencumbered by a rider.

Transitions from one pace to another, either direct or progressive, can be improved on the lunge. A good transition is one in which one good quality pace becomes another, without loss of balance, impulsion, rhythm or tempo. The voice, whip and rein aids are used as previously

described. Careful preparation must be made for each transition, ensuring that the impulsion, speed and submission are correct before applying the appropriate aids.

As his training progresses, lengthening and shortening the steps will be introduced to the horse, both of which must be achieved without hurrying or loss of balance. Working at this on the lunge is often an advantage. Working trot is established on a circle of about 16m (17yd); by gradually taking up some loops in the rein, the circle is then reduced to about 12m (13yd) – this increases the collection a little because it encourages the horse to bring his hind legs further underneath him. This increase in engagement is the basis from which all lengthening must be made. The 12m (13yd) circle is then increased again to 16m (17yd),

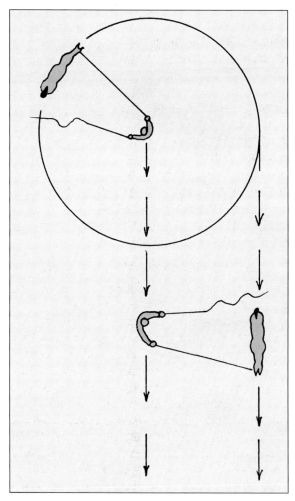

• **Fig 106** Lengthening the steps on the lunge from a 16m circle

and as the horse reaches the circumference of the 16m (17yd) circle the trainer runs forward – as shown in Fig 106 – to allow the horse to take longer steps on a straight line for about 15–20m (18–22yd). As the work improves, the number of longer steps taken can be increased. It is, of course, important to keep the horse between the whip and rein in all this work, and to work him as equally as possible on both reins.

The training exercise of 'yielding to the leg' is discussed in Chapter 5, where the horse is bent on the circumference of the circle on which he is working; this exercise can be very usefully performed on the lunge. First establish a good working trot on a 16m circle, then slowly and gradually reduce the size of the circle down to about 12m (13yd) by taking up the loops in the lunge rein. Once the 12m (13yd) circle is established, the horse is asked to step forwards and sideways, out towards the 16m (17yd) circle, by pointing the lunge whip towards his shoulder. This is good balance training, and should also help to improve agility and co-ordination (see Fig 107).

Work on the lunge need not be confined to a circle; the trainer can turn the circle into a square by walking forwards a few paces to make a straight line, and joining the straight lines together by making a quarter of a circle to form each corner. And lunge circles can be moved around the training area by the trainer walking a few steps forwards to move the centre point. Adding variety to lungeing in this way provides new challenges and helps to prevent boredom.

Lungeing the horse for work or exercise

The situation arises from time to time where the competition horse cannot be ridden for some reason, perhaps because of a minor injury that does not, however, warrant taking him off work altogether, or reducing the concentrate element of his feed. In these circumstances, he can still be given sufficient work on the lunge and be kept on full rations safely. He is fitted with his normal working tack, saddle, bridle, and protective boots. A weight cloth with 5kg (46lb) of lead may be added if it is thought necessary to increase the physical work that he will do. Together with this, the lungeing cavesson, lunge-rein and side-reins are added. After an initial warming-up period of 5 minutes or so, the side-reins are adjusted to a

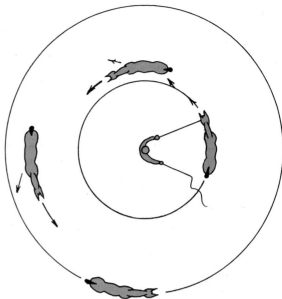

● **Fig 107** Yielding to the leg on the lunge

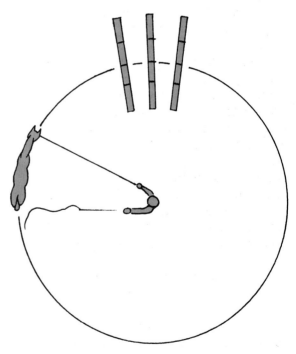

● **Fig 108** Lungeing over ground poles on a 16m circle

length that will enable him to work on the bit. It is unlikely that a horse will ever achieve useful *work* on the lunge unless he can take a bit contact through the side-reins. He can be worked on a 16m (17yd) circle in walk and trot, and on a slightly larger circle for canter. The trainer must take care to ensure that the size of the circle on which he is working is appropriate for that particular horse and is not introducing unnecessary problems. In walk and canter, where the swing of the head and neck are an important part of the correct pace, care must be taken to ensure that the side-reins do not interfere with or restrict that swing. This work can include transitions, lengthening and shortening of the steps, yielding to the leg, trotting-pole work and jumping (see Figs 106, 107, 108). The side-reins should be removed for work over trotting poles and jumping. Work on the lunge is physically demanding for the horse, and 25 to 30 minutes work would be sufficient for most fit horses; but the trainer's eye and knowledge of his horse are the only accurate guide to what is appropriate.

Riding in or warming up before a competition

Most horses react in some way when they arrive at a showground, where the presence of other horses and the various showground activities generate a degree of excitement. There are always those which are more or less unaffected, but others become tense and difficult to work with. Under these circumstances it is often more sensible to work the horse on the lunge to start with, whilst he settles. It is not always easy to find a quiet corner in which to do this, but when it can be done it allows the horse to overcome his initial excitement, and relieves the rider of the difficulties of riding him whilst he is inattentive and distracted by the unusual sights and sounds. Generally it is most convenient to dress the horse in the equipment in which he is to compete, complete with protective boots, before warming up on the lunge is started. The rider can then be dressed, ready to start mounted work as soon as the lungeing is completed, and it only remains to remove the lunge tack (and boots for some disciplines) before ridden work can start. It is usually best to start the lungeing without the side-reins connected, but the sooner they are in use the sooner real work can begin. Trot and canter can be included, together with transitions and any work that will encourage the horse to settle.

DEALING WITH EVASIONS ON THE LUNGE

If the horse's initial training has been correct and progressive, work on the lunge should present no difficulties. However, it is unrealistic to assume

that problems never occur, particularly as lungeing is often used to re-train horses that have been spoilt or that have developed particular resistances or disobediences.

A problem often encountered is that a horse refuses to lunge on his stiff side, and halts, turning in towards the trainer or even changing the rein. A possible solution is to reintroduce the assistant, who leads the horse as he would in the initial training on the lunge. This is usually successful in walk and trot for a circuit or two, but then the horse often realises that once on his own he can halt and turn in if he wants to. A sure remedy is to fit a second lunge rein to the outside ring of the cavesson, passing it through the outside stirrup iron or ring on the lungeing roller, and bringing it round behind the horse under his tail and just above the hocks. The trainer keeps a light contact on this rein so that he can feel when the pupil is about to halt or turn in, and can take the appropriate action. Patience and perseverance are required and quick results should not be expected.

Often the inattentive horse ignores the command to walk from trot or to halt from walk, in fact any downward transition. It is usually a symptom of a general lack of obedience or his ignorance of the words of command. Once again the assistant can be called in to help, but where this is not convenient a result is often achieved by leading the horse towards the fence, the wall of the school or the hedge surrounding the field as the command 'waaalk' or 'woah' is given. As he reaches the wall it becomes obvious to him that he is expected to respond. This remedy clearly has its dangers and should be used with tact and care. In serious cases the addition of the second rein, as previously described, means the trainer can apply the aids for a downward transition with both hands, which is obviously an advantage. When a positive result is achieved the horse must be rewarded with a pat on the neck and a congratulatory word.

Those that become too strong on the lunge may respond to working on a smaller circle, but they are then at greater risk of losing their balance or striking into themselves. These horses may be fitted with more severe equipment. The 'Wels' cavesson may be used, where the noseband is fitted below the bit, but it is severe and should be used with care. The lunge-rein may be fitted to the snaffle bridle as previously described, but in effect this has

● **Fig 109** Long-reining on a circle

● **Fig 110** Long-reining on the straight

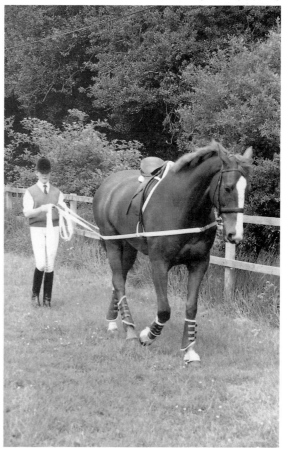

a severe gag action, and once again should be used with care.

The horse that falls in on the circle usually does so because he is working with insufficient impulsion. The trainer must make sure he is behind the horse's shoulder, driving him forwards from the voice and whip, if necessary walking on the circle. When lungeing from the centre of the circle the horse can usually be kept out on the circumference by pointing the whip at his shoulder.

LONG-REINING THE HORSE

Long-reining is a technique of dismounted training in which the trainer is able to turn the horse to the left or right and work him on straight lines (see Fig 109) in a way he cannot on the lunge. It is very useful for training the potential competition horse once he is working well on the lunge, and can in fact be used for training the advanced horse up to half-pass, piaffe, passage and flying change – here, however, it will be discussed only as training for the less specialist competition horse.

The trainer should understand that he is in a very strong position when long-reining, and that it is easy to make the horse 'overbend', and discourage him from going forwards energetically. Long-reining can be performed on a circle, which is rather like lungeing, or in straight lines, or following the school figures. When he is long-reined, other than on a circle, the work is done in walk; it is under these circumstances that the greatest care must be taken.

The same equipment is required for long-reining as for lungeing, but a second lungeing rein is necessary. A well padded lungeing roller is useful for this work, with strong rings on the side through which the long-reins pass. If a saddle is used, the stirrups must be adjusted to a height that will allow the long-reins to pass through them parallel to the ground. The stirrup irons are then tied together under the sternum to keep them steady. There are a number of techniques for long-reining, as the illustration shows; the one considered here is the normal English method.

When working on a circle, the long-reins are attached to the outside rings on the lungeing

cavesson, then pass through the stirrup irons or lungeing roller rings to the trainer. He holds one rein in each hand and the whip in the hand that is holding the outside rein. The outside rein passes round behind the horse under his tail and just above the hocks. Some horses may object to this at first, but if the equipment is handled tactfully they will soon accept the outside rein being in contact with the hind legs.

To change the rein on a circle with the long reins, the trainer takes up the outside rein to guide the horse outwards. At exactly the same time he lets out the inside rein generously, to allow the horse to come round onto the new rein. If the trainer is sufficiently agile this exercise can be done in walk and trot. (See Fig 111.)

Fig 112 shows a series of 'serpentine' loops, a good suppling exercise that can be made on the long-reins.

The horse can be long-reined over a series of poles at trot or walk. For the average horse in trot the poles should be between 1.20 to 1.40m (4–5ft) apart, but should be adjusted to suit the individual horse. (See Fig 113).

Long-reining on straight lines can be a most rewarding method of training, and it is here that the

● **Fig 111** Changing the rein on long-reins

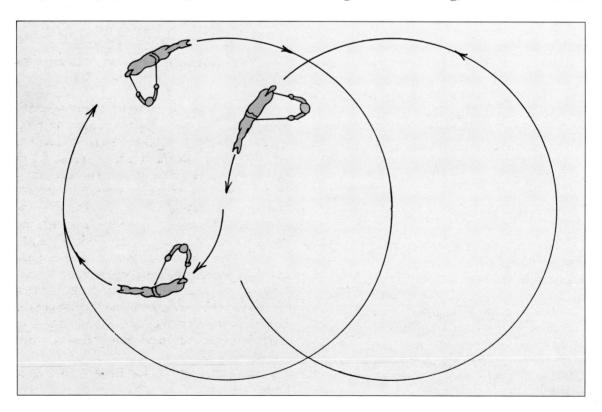

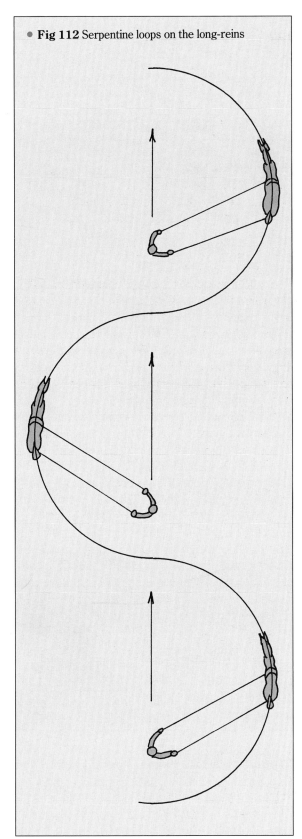

• **Fig 112** Serpentine loops on the long-reins

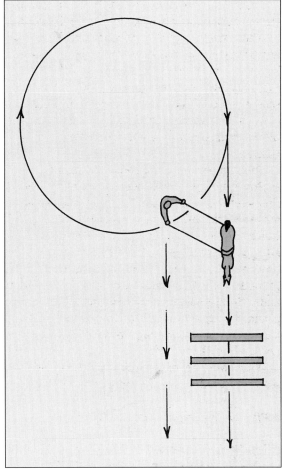

• **Fig 113** Long-reining over ground poles from a 16m circle

real advantage of long-reining over lungeing can be seen, as the trainer now has control over the direction in which the horse is going. It is a useful technique for introducing horses to many situations before they are backed. They can be long-reined on the road and through the village, along the bridleway and through the woods and fields, and generally be introduced to the sights, sounds and hazards of every-day life. As this work can only be done in walk, the trainer must ensure that the horse is allowed complete freedom to go energetically forward, and is allowed enough rein to adjust the height of his head and the length of his neck as he wishes. It is easy to get the horse 'overbent' or 'behind the bit' unintentionally, both of which should be avoided.

Training the rider on the lunge is covered in Chapter 9.

TRAINING THE COMPETITION RIDER

There are a number of qualities required by the successful competition rider that are common to other sports. It is the duty of the trainer to develop and encourage these qualities where they exist, and to try to establish them where they are not obviously apparent.

PHYSICAL SUITABILITY AND FITNESS

The good competition rider must have the nerve of a downhill skier, the balance, agility, suppleness and co-ordination of the gymnast, the endurance of a middle-distance runner, and the rhythm, grace and showmanship of the ballet dancer.

Most of these qualities can be developed by progressive, intelligent training, but there is undoubtedly a certain quality which some people possess in either a plus or a minus quantity that makes them a 'natural' on a horse or (in the worst cases) a 'liability'. As a minus quantity, the effect on the horse is difficult to overcome; as a plus quantity the results of good training can be very rewarding. It is not necessarily true that 'good horsemen are born and not made', but in more recent times the likes of Lester Piggot and Mark Todd have shown that they have some innate quality that is not bestowed on all.

Whilst a calm, relaxed rider will, in time, relax and quieten a tense horse, a tense, nervous rider will instantly transmit his own nervousness and tension to a sensitive horse – some seem to have an apparently 'electric' seat and manage to make even the most placid horse nervous.

Success in any competitive sport depends to a large degree on the dedication and singlemindedness of the competitor. But in competition riding, devotion to the horse on a year-round basis is a fundamental requirement. Skis can be put into store when the snow has gone and tennis racquets put away out of season, but the horse must be cared for all the year round, even when he is out at grass at rest. Dedication to his feeding, veterinary care, equipment and general well-being are a duty from which the horse-owner is never relieved. A competition rider who is not prepared to dedicate himself to these chores will be limited in his potential as a gold medallist.

Many competitive sports require the participant to have 'a good eye' and a keen attention to detail: competition riding requires this quality to a very high degree. An analytical approach is required not only to riding technique in the dressage arena and on the jumping course, but also to feeding, shoeing, saddlery, bitting, soundness, veterinary care and every aspect of the horse's care and work.

The conformation of the competition rider is important in as much as it inevitably dictates his effectiveness as a horseman – although from time to time, champion riders of most unlikely proportions are found. However, the ballet school, for example, will not accept young people for training if the physique of the potential pupil does not conform to that required by the school. This has never been the case in riding, but there are, nonetheless, features of human conformation that make the rider more, or less, easy to train.

Many men of 1.83m (6ft) and over ride, and a few become expert, but a limiting factor is the number of quality horses big enough to carry them,

• **Fig 114** Elegance and presence are important in the dressage horse

particularly if they weigh 75kg (165lb) or over. It is never flattering to look 'underhorsed'. In a similar vein, any competitor under 1.68m (6ft) in height and weighing 63kg (139lb) or more may have difficulty in presenting an elegant picture. Short fat thighs, an over-heavy upper body and the absence of a neck leave a rider at a certain disadvantage both in appearance, and probably in effectiveness as well. For a rider to be overweight is unacceptable. To carry 5kg (46lb) of spare fat is a considerable handicap, and no competition gymnast, runner or tennis player would even consider it – but in competition riding this is not an uncommon sight.

Being overweight can, of course, be a medical condition which is difficult to correct, but as a rule it *can* be controlled by self-discipline and diet. As much as it is incompetent and unfair to the horse to complete a phase of the speed and endurance day 30 seconds faster than the time allowed, it is equally unfair and incompetent to expect the horse to carry appreciably more weight than the minimum laid down by the rules.

The physical fitness of the competition rider is of

paramount importance. A good cardio-vascular system is essential to ensure that the rider can be effective and balanced at the end of the seventeen kilometers of speed and endurance day: the horse must not be left to fend for himself over the last one thousand metres of phase 'D' because the rider is too exhausted to be anything but a passenger.

The techniques of balance, agility and co-ordination must be developed in the competition rider, and the fundamental ingredient in these is suppleness. Also, a nervous rider is by definition tense, since the muscles are contracted in anticipation of the horse doing something unexpected. Suppleness is therefore related to confidence, in a way. Riders are frequently stiff where the leg joins the body, the large joint where the top of the femur fits into the pelvis, and this detracts from their ability to sit deep in the saddle with a soft seat. Stiffness in the neck and shoulders results in unsteady hands and forearms; stiffness in the back inhibits their ability to swing the hips softly in unison with the swing of the horse's back.

The person who rides one or two horses a day on a serious training programme probably keeps himself sufficiently fit to compete competently. And although dismounted physical training is thoroughly commendable, no amount will compensate for insufficient mounted training. Dismounted physical training will certainly complement mounted training provided that it is carried out conscientiously and on a regular basis. Jogging and general suppling exercises carried out daily can maintain good wind and suppleness, not only in those who are unable to ride daily, but also for those who ride every day. A series of recommended exercises is shown in Figs 115–28.

There are individual skills that the competition rider must master to become truly effective. At first the trainer can be of assistance, but ultimately the rider must be responsible for them himself. These are his general philosophy and attitude towards the horse; his posture and position in the saddle; his ability to ride the dressage test and walk the jumping courses with skill and forethought; and to judge pace across country and in the showjumping arena.

• **Fig 115** Arm circling
• **Fig 116** Arm circling forwards and backwards to improve suppleness in the shoulders

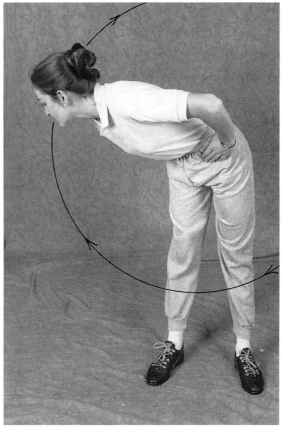

• **Figs 117-19** Trunk circling

• **Figs 120-2** Stretching exercises

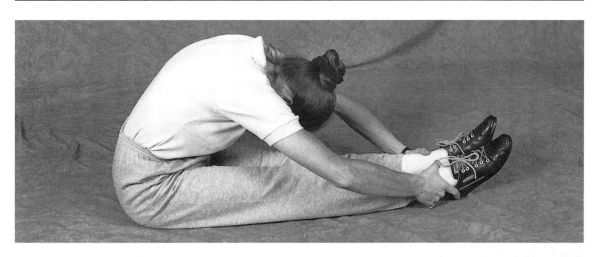

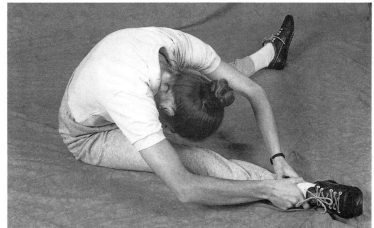

• **Figs 123-5** Stretching exercises

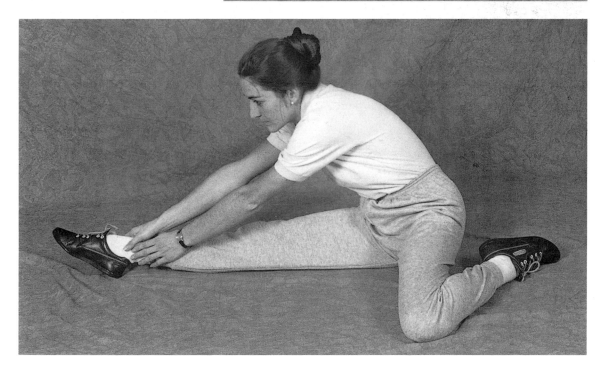

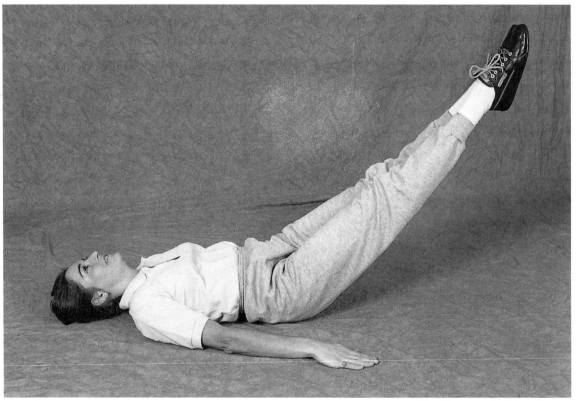

GENERAL PHILOSOPHY

- **Fig 126** (top left) Stretching exercise
- **Fig 127** (bottom left) Strengthening the stomach muscles
- **Fig 128** (above) Strengthening the thigh muscles

It is important for a potential competition rider to study a particular school of training in depth and to stick to that school until his physical ability and his understanding of what is required are well established. It makes little difference which school is studied – German, Viennese, French, Scandinavian, English – as, with the exception of some esoteric schools, their eventual aims are similar. To read, in the early stages, all the written works that are available can be confusing and misleading. It is not until one set of training principles is clearly established that elements from other schools of thought can be recognised and evaluated to advantage.

No matter which school is studied, the competition rider must understand the basic requirements of training the competition horse:

1. The horse must go willingly forwards with energy and without resistance. The term 'go forwards', in horse training, means more than just progressing in a forward direction by putting one foot in front of the other: his whole purpose, both physical and mental, must be to go energetically forwards. 'Without resistance' means that he is co-operating with his rider and is not showing any sign of disobeying by napping, rearing, bucking, grinding his teeth, swishing his tail, or simply not trying to do what he is being asked to do.

2. He must be straight: that is, 'straight' on straight lines and bent throughout his length (or as near as is anatomically possible) on the circumference of a circle or the curve of a corner. At times the horse may, as an evasion, go crookedly perhaps by swinging his hind quarters out to the left or right to avoid doing what he is being asked to do. Under these circumstances he is crooked, which is a bad fault.

3. He must work in a sure, steady rhythm and in an even tempo in each of his basic paces.

4. He must work in 'self-carriage': that is, in his own balance – he must not lean on the rider's hands through the reins and the bit.

5. The horse must learn to work well 'on the bit'.

6. When working to the right he must bend to the right, and when working to the left he must bend to the left.

LIBRARY
DISHOP BURTON COLLEGE
DEVERLEY HU17 8QG

125

If these basic rules of training are not clearly in the rider's mind he will not be able to train and ride his horse in competition to the best of their joint ability.

Much can be learned from the close study of experts performing in their own particular disciplines, and both the advantages and the disadvantages of their techniques can often be recognised by the astute observer. Also, watching and studying competitors in the lower echelons of competition often helps to identify and correct faults that exist in one's own work. An observant and analytical approach to training should be encouraged in all competition riders.

It is difficult to work with and to train horses without making a study, even subconciously, of their behaviour and the ways in which the individual horse might react in certain circumstances. A close study of horse behaviour/psychology is a vital part of extracting the best from any horse; to ignore it is to invite unexpected reactions in moments of stress and difficulty.

POSTURE AND POSITION

Not many human beings in the civilised world can be described as straight, elegant movers. Due to the influences of modern living – badly designed seating, beds and shoes; bad carrying and lifting techniques; and a general lack of deportment training – crooked, unbalanced movers are common, and those that are crooked and unbalanced on the ground are unlikely to be straight and balanced on the horse. Furthermore, the competition rider must be convinced that sitting correctly is fundamental to having a good effect on his horse; and the reasons for sitting correctly should be taught in the first few riding lessons. They are important then, and they become increasingly important as the level of riding and competing rises. The reasons for sitting correctly are:

1   A correct riding position gives the horse a well balanced load to carry. A well balanced load is easier to carry than an unbalanced load.
2   A correct position enables the rider to apply the aids with the legs, hands and seat quickly and effectively.
3   A correct position enables the rider to look his most elegant. If the horse is expected to look

supple, balanced and elegant the rider must surely be the same.

The rider's position varies between the equestrian disciplines, but all the variations stem from a basically correct seat. To establish this seat, the following points are important:

1   The rider must sit fully in the bottom of the saddle with equal weight on each seat bone, leaning neither to the right nor to the left. The weight should be on the seat, and not on the stirrups, knees or the inside of the rider's thighs. This means the seat can be independent, with the hands and legs able to be used individually. The hips and shoulders should be straight to the front. To carry one hip or shoulder forwards or backwards unbalances the load, and an unbalanced load will cause the horse to make an adjustment in his way of going, perhaps making him crooked and causing uneven wear on joints and tendons. It may even set up a resistance of some sort.
2   The body should be upright without being stiff, the body weight being directly over the seat. A plumb-line dropped from the rider's ear should pass down through his shoulder, and through the hip to the heel. The shape of the upper body is important: essentially it should be the natural shape of the rider, but this can be enhanced by encouraging him/her to lift the chest, stretching the distance from the bottom rib to the hip bone so that the abdomen is long and flat and not short and round. The shoulder blades should be softly closed together behind the rider. It is, of course, important that none of these corrections introduces stiffness.
3   The head is a big, heavy, influential part of the rider's body, and where it goes, the body tends to follow. The gymnast, the high-board diver and the ballet dancer start the movement of the body by a movement of the head. It follows that the competent rider must be in control of the position of his head. The neck should come out from between the shoulders, and not from where the knot of the tie would normally be. The head should be carried at a height naturally correct for the rider, not too high as this creates tension, but certainly not looking down at the wither. The rider should look straight to

• **Fig 129** A very
good, balanced
position in the
dressage saddle

the front, pointing his nose and chin between the horse's ears. This does not mean that he may never look to the left or to the right, but it does mean that he should not look permanently left or right, as this will affect the balance of his body. Many riders when concentrating on their work will, if not corrected, ride looking down or with the head on one side.

4 The muscles controlling the joint where the femur fits into the pelvis must be relaxed in order that the leg may be softly wrapped around the horse without gripping (though gripping with the leg must be taught eventu-

ally). The leg should hang so that as much of the inside as possible is in contact with the saddle and the horse's side. The ball of the foot should be on the stirrup iron, with the heel slightly lower than the toe; the rider's knee-cap and the toe of his boot point directly to the front; the stirrup leather should hang vertically.

This attitude of the leg enables the rider to apply the aids quickly and effectively. It also enables him to ride with a still leg, and the rider with still legs encourages the horse to respond to light leg aids: legs that move continually result in the horse ignoring the leg aids, which then have to be made more vigorously in order to have an effect.

The position of the rider's legs has an effect on the upper part of the body, and a correct leg position helps the upper body to remain upright. If the lower leg is carried too far forwards, the upper body tends to tip backwards; if the lower leg is carried too far back, the upper body tends to tip forwards. Both of these faults detract from the effectiveness of the rider.

5 The hands should be held in front of the body in a workmanlike position, neither too high nor too low. The experienced horse trainer will be able to adjust the height of his hands to suit a particular situation. They should be an even pair, the same height above the wither and the same distance either side, with the thumbs on top and the knuckles to the outside.

The reins are held surely in the fingers but without excessive grip. Under normal circumstances it should be possible to draw an imaginary straight line from the rider's elbow down the forearm, through the little finger to the bit in the horse's mouth. As the rider looks down on his forearm he should see a straight line down his arm, along the thumb and down the rein to the bit. This helps to establish how far apart the hands should be carried. The upper arm and elbow fall softly against the rider's side so that the inside of the sleeve brushes the side of the jacket; the elbows should not be clamped down tight against the side. In order that the horse can be ridden 'on the bit' and 'between the leg and hand' the reins must be of a suitable length for a particular horse and his stage of training. In the trained rider it is a matter of personal choice, but in general the reins must be short enough for him to maintain a sure, steady, even contact on the horse's mouth. They must not be so short that there is no bend in the elbow, and they must not be so long that the elbows come behind the rider's back.

This basic position is adjusted for some schooling, and for jumping and fast cross-country work.

When training the young horse the stirrups are a little shorter so the weight is not taken directly on his back; otherwise the same principles apply.

For jumping, during training and in competition, the stirrups are shortened so the rider can lift the seat out of the saddle, distributing his bodyweight between his knees and his stirrups. This is necessary if he is to lower his centre of gravity towards the horse, allowing the horse full use of his back when galloping and jumping, and enabling the rider to go forward with him, staying in balance throughout the process of the jump. A guide to the number of holes that the stirrups should be shortened is that the rider's knee should fit snugly into the knee-rolls on the saddle. It is a mistake to shorten them so much that the knee comes above the roll, or to have them so long that the knee-roll is not being correctly used. (This theory presupposes that the saddle is the correct size for the rider in the first place.) The other aspects of the basic position remain the same, ie the attitude of the head, the shape of the upper body, the position of the legs, feet, hands, and arms.

Establishing a correct seat takes time and supervised practice. Undoubtedly the most convincing way of showing a rider what he should do is to record his work on video tape. No amount of verbal explanation and correction can be as effective as actually showing the pupil what he is doing on a

• **Fig 130** Shortened stirrups enable the rider to stay in balance at fast paces and when jumping

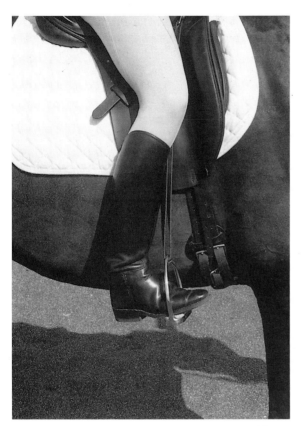

● **Fig 131** The correct attitude of the lower leg and foot

● **Fig 132** The lower leg drawn back to apply the canter or hind quarter controlling aid

moving picture. Discussion is important, and is particularly valuable when a group of riders are training together. Video recordings used in these discussions can help a great deal in identifying strengths and weaknesses in both horses and riders and in helping to rectify problems.

Some riding schools are fitted with mirrors on the walls of one long, and one short side. They are particularly useful to the rider who works on his own, and he should be encouraged to use them. They provide a good view of both horse and rider as they pass down one long side, and are particularly useful if one is placed on the short side directly at the end of the track, so that the rider can check on his straightness as he rides up the track.

Understanding the aids

The rider has only a few aids at his disposal to ask the horse to carry out a very wide range of activities. He can use his legs, seat, hands and voice, or a combination of all four: these are known as the 'natural' aids. To make the natural aids more effective he may use what are known as the 'artificial' aids, the whip and the spur. The trainer can tell the rider which aids, or combination of aids, should be used to achieve a particular result. It is then for the rider to use his 'feel' and imagination to blend those aids in a way that will achieve the desired result with any particular horse. No two horses are identical and their response to the various aids varies widely.

The Leg-aids: The inside leg (the leg on the inside of the bend of the horse), used directly inwards, and with the stirrup leather hanging vertically, asks the horse to go forwards, and it is important that he is trained to respond to this aid if an advanced degree of training is to be achieved. There will be times when the horse must be driven energetically forwards with both legs used together, perhaps when he is tempted to refuse at a jump or when opposing polo players are chasing the ball together. The outside leg is the leg that con-

• **Fig 133** The reins of the snaffle bridle (above) and the double bridle (below) correctly held

trols the hind quarters and prevents them from swinging out. It is also the leg that asks the horse to canter, although it should be noted that in some schools the canter aid is applied with the inside leg. The principle of applying the leg-aids is *not* that by kicking the horse's sides vigorously so much pain is inflicted that he goes forward to avoid it, but a clear means of polite communication between rider and horse. Quick, sharp leg-aids usually get a quick response, slow dull leg-aids get a slow dull response. The aim of the aids should be to get the maximum response from the horse from minimum effort on the part of the rider. It therefore follows that once a leg-aid is effective, the rider should aim to reduce it whilst maintaining its effectiveness.

Back-, seat-, or weight-aids: These are different terms which in effect mean the same thing. The rider can, and must, use his 'body-weight' as an aid to encourage the horse forwards; he uses his bodyweight through his 'seat'; and to enable the weight to be transmitted to the horse through the seat, the muscles of the 'back' must be used. This aid can only be productively used when the rider has a deep supple seat. The rider who sits incorrectly – on the back of the saddle, crookedly, or to one side – and uses his seat strongly, will have an adverse effect on the horse's way of going. Only when the horse is working on the bit, in a good outline and with the back rounded can the seat aids be correctly applied. Driving with the seat on a hollow horse only serves to make him more hollow.

The hands: Some riders are said to be born with good hands. This may be so, but with skilled training and diligent application, any rider's hands can be improved to an acceptable standard. The outside hand (the hand on the outside of the bend of the horse) receives, guides and controls the impulsion created by the inside leg. It also controls the speed of the horse and the bend in the neck. The inside hand (the hand on the inside of the bend) asks the horse to look in the direction in which he is going. It is a slight misnomer to refer to these aids as 'hand-aids', as they are in fact applied by subtle squeezes with the fingers. In cases of extreme emergency, of course, it is necessary to pull with one hand or the other (never both together) to stop the horse. But by this time the normal means of communication will, temporarily, have broken down.

Training on the lunge

• **Fig 134** A suppling exercise: arm circling on the lunge

All riders, whatever the level they are working at, benefit from regular tuition on the lunge. A lunge lesson once a month would help to keep a competition rider correct in his posture and, if the appropriate horse and trainer were available, would help him to make progress in his ridden work.

Training on the lunge helps the competition rider to maintain a deep supple seat, to lengthen and correct the attitude of the leg, and to learn to sit softly on the advanced horse, which has greater and more elevated movement than the novice horse. It is a prerequisite of this training that an advanced 'schoolmaster' horse and an experienced trainer are available.

Whilst safety is of paramount importance, it should not be necessary for the rider to have reins or stirrups for this work. The rider should have the experience and confidence to sit on the horse, the horse should be obedient and trained to an advanced level (if it is not, then it is not suitable for this work), and the trainer should be competent in lungeing (if he is not, then he is unlikely to be able to help the rider). The purpose of lungeing the rider is mainly to improve the depth of the seat, and

• **Fig 135** Exercise on the lunge: one finger of each hand lightly looped under the pommel to help the rider to sit deeper in the saddle

● **Fig 136** Trunk twisting on the lunge, another exercise to aid suppleness

if in those moments when he feels he is losing his balance he resorts to the stirrups for security, then the lunge work is wasted. Likewise it should not be necessary for him to secure himself in the saddle by holding on to the reins. There are some riders who can ride with an adequately long leg without stirrups, but have difficulty maintaining that length with stirrups; it may help these riders to be lunged with stirrups from time to time.

The horse should be dressed as for normal lungeing, but with a dressage saddle. Little help can be given to an advanced rider on the lunge in a forward-cut saddle, as it is too long and too shallow in the seat, and too short in the flap to help the rider to sit in a correct dressage seat.

There are a number of exercises that can be helpful in relieving the rider of positional faults: see Figs 134–6. Other exercises are available to improve suppleness, but as a rule these are best done dismounted. The most useful work for the competition rider is that which helps him to feel what is happening underneath him, and helps him to blend the movement of his body into that of the horse's back without making *more* movement than the horse makes for him. To achieve this, the trainer must be able to lunge the horse in collection, and from that collection be able, for example, to lengthen the steps towards medium trot or canter so that the rider can learn to go with, and absorb the change of spring in the step. It is important that the trainer keeps the lunge horse working in a steady tempo so that the rider can learn the significance of rhythm and tempo in walk, trot and canter. Transitions correctly made on the lunge can help the rider to execute them well when he is riding free.

RIDING THE DRESSAGE TEST

The purpose of the competition dressage test is to show off the horse's natural paces, and the way those paces and his natural balance have been trained to carry a rider. It is not sufficient simply to follow, mechanically, the movements in the test even if this is with accuracy and without actually going wrong. In a good test there is an element of 'dash' just as there is in a good cross-country round, and the talented dressage rider can show off the horse's strengths and hide, to a degree, his weaknesses. With this in mind, the competition dressage rider must develop a sense of showmanship and be able to stage-manage his test.

Planning and preparation are vital elements in riding a good test. Feeding, grooming, plaiting, shoeing, fitting studs, checking equipment for both horse and rider, checking transport, travelling time and 'start-times' and, above all, learning the test, may all contribute to success or failure. The competitor who arrives at the showground late, hot and flustered with insufficient time to ride in as he normally would, creates unnecessary difficulties for himself. Depending on the amount of riding in that the horse requires, a minimum of one hour, better two, should be allowed between arriving at the showground and riding the test. It is always an advantage to have a competent assistant to help with administration, tacking-up etc, leaving the competitor to concentrate solely on riding in and competing.

A typical Elementary test

Once the rider's number is called, he should ride around the outside of the arena close to the markers and the judge's stand or car, to allow the horse to see any strange sights that may be present. For at least the final part of this exercise he should be going at the pace at which he is to enter the arena. When the signal is made for him to enter and start, he must do so within 60 seconds.

It may be necessary to complete a circuit outside the arena, and it is important to go some 15 metres (16yd) away from the 'A' marker at the entrance (or as far as is conveniently possible) to ensure a straight entrance: to make a sharp turn into the arena will make riding straight down the 'A' to 'C' line very difficult.

1 'A'. Enter at working trot.
'X'. Halt, Salute. Proceed at working trot.

After the entry at 'A', the 'C' marker should be kept directly between the horse's ears, and the rider, whilst looking for 'E' and 'B' to locate 'X', should establish 'eye contact' with the judge. No judge is impressed by a rider who, through lack of confidence or good manners, ignores him. As he approaches 'X' he makes the necessary half-halts, drops the seat softly into the saddle, closes on both legs, and asks for halt with the minimum feel of the fingers, halting square and exactly at 'X'. He maintains the contact with both the legs and hands to keep the horse attentive and on the bit at halt. He salutes (see pp 68–9), takes a rein in each hand, and rides directly forwards in working trot. Before reaching 'C' he shows both the horse and the judge that at 'C' a turn is to be made to the left, by bending the horse slightly left whilst continuing to go straight towards 'C'.

2 'C'. Track left.
'E'. Turn left.
'B'. Track right.

At this level, the right-angle turns and corners, depending on the suppleness of the horse, should be a quarter of an 8-metre circle or slightly less. Thus the movement from the centre line to the 'E' side of the arena should not be a half 10-metre circle, but should include a few steps straight along the 'C' short side. Half-halts, where necessary, are made prior to each corner. The left turn at 'E', preceded by a half-halt, should start about 4 metres before the 'E' marker so that he can make a quarter of an 8-metre circle and end it straight, on the 'E' to 'B' line. As the 'X' marker is crossed, the bend is changed, and the right turn started about 4 metres before 'B' so that a quarter of an 8-metre circle can be made to finish on the track on the right rein, just past 'B'. The important points in riding this figure are that the 'E' to 'B' line should be straight, and as long as possible without causing loss of balance or shortening of the steps at 'E' or 'B' by turning too abruptly.

3 **'K'. Circle right 10-metre diameter.**
Half-halts are made between 'A' and 'K' and the bend established to ensure that the 10-metre circle can be accurately ridden. Care is taken to ride a good 'A' to 'K' corner, and the circle is started at 'K'. It should touch the centre line with one step at 'D' and be one metre in from the 'A' short side, finishing exactly at 'K'. The working trot tempo must be maintained through the corner and on the circle; loss or variation of tempo may indicate to the judge that the horse is stiff on that rein, which should be avoided.

4 **'E'–'X'.   Half-circle   right   10-metre diameter.**
'X'–'B'. Half-circle left 10-metre diameter.
These two half-circles must be made in the same way as a full circle, with the appropriate bend and well maintained tempo. Only one straight step is allowed at 'X' during which the bend is changed to ensure a good half-circle to the left, but be sure of making that one straight step at 'X' to ensure that the last half-circle is correctly finished and the new one correctly started. It is a mistake, obvious to the judge, to cross the centre line at 'X', between the two half-circles, at an angle.

5 **'M'. Circle left 10-metre diameter.**
The same principles apply here as they do in the 10-metre circle to the right. This circle is followed by medium trot, so it is a good opportunity to ensure that the hind legs are well engaged and that there is sufficient impulsion to make the longer steps.

6 **'H'–'E'–'K'. Medium trot.**
'K'–'A'–'F'. Working trot.
If sufficient impulsion has been built up on the 10-metre circle and maintained around the 'C' end of the arena, with a good corner at 'M' to 'C' and at 'C' to 'H' the horse should be in a good position to make medium trot from 'H' to 'K'. The object should be to make two good transitions, working to medium trot at 'H' and medium to working trot at 'K': the horse should not be allowed to run into medium nor fall onto the forehand back into working trot. Good impulsion in the 'C' to 'H' corner will allow a good transition to medium at 'H', and maintaining tempo and balance by using half-halts in the medium will enable a good transi-tion back to working trot at 'K'.

The period in working trot from 'K' to 'F' should be used to recover any balance that may have been lost in the medium trot. The trot tempo should be checked, and two good corners ridden with a *straight* short side through 'A'. 'K' to 'F' should be used to build up the impulsion, by the use of half-halts, for the medium trot in the next movement.

7 **'F'–'X'–'H'. Change the rein at medium trot.**
'H'. Working trot.
The medium trot across the diagonal is slightly more difficult than down the long side, as there are no boards to guide the horse. The same principles apply for preparing for medium trot, ie the impulsion must be sufficient for him to spring into medium steps as soon as he is asked to do so. If there is insufficient engage-ment of the hind legs when he is asked to lengthen he will only be able to run faster on his forehand, which will gain poor marks. In order to go straight from 'F' to 'H' the rider should see the 'H' marker clearly between the horse's ears. As he turns off the track at 'F' he allows with the hands and asks for medium trot with the seat and legs, showing a good transition from working to medium. Just after 'X' he probably needs to make a half-halt or two to ensure that he can make a good transition from medium to working trot as he reaches 'H'. The transitions within the pace are an important part of the test, and their quality will be re-flected in the mark for the movement.

8 **'C'. Halt. Immobility 6 seconds.**
Proceed at medium walk.
The 'H' to 'C' corner must be used to ensure, by the use of the half-halt, that the horse is sufficiently well balanced to halt from working trot at 'C', and the rider should aim to halt with his shoulder exactly level with the 'C' marker. Once again the halt should be square, steady, attentive and on the bit. The horse must be kept between the leg and hand ready to move off in medium walk at the end of the 6-second halt (most riders find it necessary actually to count up to six at halt to get the timing exactly right). The rider's inside leg, away from the judge, can be used to ensure that he keeps the horse's attention at halt and that he is ready to

Fig 137 A 10m circle in the 'C'–'H' corner

step off when asked to do so. The first step in walk should be a full bold step and the four-time rhythm should be picked up immediately. An accurate, round corner should be ridden between 'C' and 'M'.

9 'M'–'X'–'K'. Change rein at free walk on a long rein.
'K'. Medium walk.

After 'M' the rider must set his sights clearly on the 'K' marker to ensure that the change of rein is made on a straight line. Both reins are let out to their full length to ask the horse to stretch his head and neck forward and down. The rider's hands can be carried low, on either side of the wither to encourage this. Tactful contact must be kept with the legs, and the seat allowed to swing in rhythm with the swing of the horse's back, in order that the steps can be long, regular and purposeful. As he approaches 'K' the reins are taken up tactfully and medium walk established. Between 'K' and 'A' preparations are made for canter, ie the bend to the left is checked or re-established by the inside leg and the fingers of the inside hand. The impulsion is ensured with the seat and inside leg.

10 Before 'A'. Working canter.
'F'–'B'–'M'. Two loops, each loop to be 2m diameter in from the track and touching at 'B'.

If the preparations after 'K' have been well made, it should only be necessary to keep the body upright, drop the seat softly into the saddle, and bring back the outside leg to ask for canter. The 'A' to 'F' corner, made in canter, may be a little rounder than in trot at this level, perhaps a quarter circle between 8 and 9 metres diameter. The loops are made to show a few steps towards counter canter when returning to the track. They should not be greater than 2 metres and should be made softly guiding the horse with a combination of leg-, seat- and hand-aids. It helps if the rider looks positively in the direction in which he is going. The loops should be even and smooth, the end of the first loop and the start of the second loop just touching the track at 'B'.

11 'C'. Circle left 15m diameter.

After the serpentine loops, half-halts are made between 'M' and 'C' in preparation for the 15-metre canter circle at 'C'. This circle is exactly in front of the judge who gets a very close view of what is happening. The canter must be a little on the collected side of working, and the circle must be exactly 15 metres diameter. This means that the first tangent point is at 'C' where the circle starts, the next is 2.5 metres in from the track on the 'E' side, the next is 2.5 metres in from 'X' and the last 2.5 metres in from the track on the 'B' side of the arena. It is most accurate if the circle is ridden as four separate quarters, the rider aiming to ride from tangent point to tangent point and making the same number of steps on each quarter circle.

12 'H'–'X'–'F'. Change the rein with a change of leg through trot at 'X'.

Here, once again, the line 'H' to 'F' must be ridden straight by keeping the 'F' marker between the horse's ears. The downward transition to trot is started shortly after leaving 'H' to ensure two or three good trot steps before 'X' and two or three after. During the trot steps the change of bend must be made to ensure a good upward transition to canter so that he can reach 'F' balanced and bent in the direction in which he is going. The 'F' to 'A' corner is used to prepare for the 15-metre circle at 'A'.

13 'A'. Circle right 15m diameter.

The same principles apply to riding this circle as those that apply to riding the previous 15-metre circle. Most horses prefer one canter lead to the other and often it is the right lead that is found more difficult. If this is so, it may be necessary to keep the outside leg back a little, towards the canter aid, to ensure that the canter right is maintained enthusiastically by the horse.

14 'K'–'E'–'H'. Two loops, each 2m in from the track, touching the track at 'E'.

The same principles apply to riding these loops as those that apply on the left rein.

15 'B'. Turn right.
'X'. Simple change of leg.
'E'. Track left.

The simple change of leg at elementary level may be made with a progressive transition canter–trot–walk, but the upward transition walk to canter must be direct.

• **Fig 138** In 'free walk on a long rein' this horse should be taking more rein

The distance from 'B' to 'E' is 20 metres, giving only limited room for this movement. To ensure a good transition from canter to trot it should be started a metre or two before 'B', and the turn at 'B' used to help the transition. This will help to make a balanced working trot a few steps before 'X' where the horse must walk for three steps in preparation for canter left. The importance of the tactful use of the half-halt throughout this exercise cannot be over-emphasised.

At the end of the walk steps, the bend and impulsion should be exactly right for him to strike off into canter when the rider asks by bringing back his outside leg. It is in these circumstances that the principle of reducing the aids to the minimum to achieve a desired response, is most appreciated. A balanced left turn is made by starting a quarter 8-metre circle about 4 metres before the 'E' marker. Between 'E' and 'K' half-halts are made, if necessary, to enable a good transition to be made at 'K'.

'K'. Working trot.
'A'. Down the centre line.
'X'. Medium walk.
'G'. Halt. Salute.
Leave arena at walk on a long rein at 'A'.
The transition to trot is made by dropping the seat softly into the saddle, closing on both legs to ensure engagement of the horse's hind legs, and asking for trot by the minimum feel of the fingers of the outside hand. A good corner is ridden after 'K' and the rider glances down the centre line to ensure that he is going to be central after his left turn at 'A'. Half-halts between 'A' and 'X' ensure a purposeful transition to medium walk at 'X' and a further transition to halt at 'G'. The same principles apply at the final halt as at the first halt: the horse must be square, attentive and on the bit. After the final salute, as he moves off, the reins are let out long, he turns left or right at 'C' and from the next quarter marker, 'M' or 'H', walks on a long rein directly towards, and out of the exit at 'A'. The test does not finish until the horse has left the arena at 'A', therefore jogging, coming above the bit or any other deviation from 'free walk on a long rein' will be penalised.

TEACHING THE COMPETITION RIDER PACE JUDGEMENT

Almost all jumping competitions, both showjumping and cross-country, are eventually decided on time. The speed required in novice competitions is comparatively slow, but it increases as the standard of the competition rises. Some showjumping competitions are decided on time alone. Once the course builder has designed and measured his course he can, by reference to the speed required for the competition (which is laid down in the rules), decide on two 'times': one is 'the time allowed', ie the time the competitor is allowed in which to complete the course, after which 'time faults' are incurred; the second is the 'time limit' (usually twice the 'time allowed') after which the competitor is eliminated. Both these times are indicated on the course plan which is available to all competitors well in advance of the start of the class.

It is incompetent and unprofessional for a competitor to complete the course very much faster than the 'time allowed', as it not only risks hitting the fences and incurring faults, but it takes more out of the horse than is necessary, putting him at a disadvantage in the jump-off, or in further classes that day, or in the next phase in a combined training event. It is equally incompetent and unprofessional to jump a clear round and by carelessness or bad judgement of pace, incur half a time fault and consequently lose first place.

Training a competition horse for a period of many weeks, and over very many miles, subjects it to considerable and unnatural strain. This strain will be aggravated if the rider does not have a good understanding of pace judgement, and if he fails to assess how fast he is going with some degree of accuracy. From this it will be appreciated that a competition rider must be trained, not only to be aware of the speed required for a particular class, but to be able to ride his horse at that speed.

The range of speeds required throughout the equestrian disciplines is wide. In horse trials, the speed required for phases 'A' and 'C' (the roads and tracks) of a three day event is 220 metres (240yd)

● **Fig 139** Horse and rider going well cross-country

per minute; phase 'B', the steeplechase, is 690 metres (754yd) per minute; phase 'D', the cross-country phase, is up to 570 metres (623yd) per minute. In showjumping, the speed required can be from 300 metres (328yd) per minute for some junior classes up to 400 metres (437yd) per minute for advanced adult classes.

There are a number of ways to help a competition rider develop good pace judgement. The first option is to let him go out and compete and learn by trial and error; this is the usual course taken by the self-taught competitor. Where a trainer has influence over a rider, the method could well be interval training over measured courses, because it is a very effective way of instilling this skill. Galloping alongside an experienced competitor on an experienced horse can be helpful. Some training areas are laid out in such a way that the competitor can gallop alongside a car driven at the appropriate speed. This technique can be accurate, but the facilities are seldom available.

In showjumping competitions and hunter trials where only one speed is required, the rider must be able to judge his own speed around the course. Remember, however, that the trainer or assistant stationed around the course to give time checks is giving 'outside assistance' which is contrary to the rules and may incur elimination.

All horse-trials riders ride the speed and endurance with one or more stop-watches so they can keep a check on their progress throughout the day. Many make out a card with kilometer checkpoints listed on it, together with their expected time of arrival at each point, and tape it to the forearm where it can be seen easily and used in conjunction with the stop-watch.

WALKING THE JUMPING COURSES

Jumping competitions are sometimes won by a competitor who has walked the course more thoroughly than the others, and are frequently lost by those who have not walked the course sufficiently well. It is therefore essential in both showjumping and cross-country competitions for the rider to know exactly which route he is going to take and how he will approach each of the obstacles on the course.

The showjumping course

Before a showjumping class starts, the course plan is usually displayed in the collecting ring for all competitors to study prior to walking the course. This plan shows not only the plan of the fences, but also the table under which the class will be held – the speed required in metres per minute, the time allowed, the time limit, and the jump-off course. This is all vital information that the competitor requires before he walks the course.

When walking the course, notice where the judges' box is situated, and exactly where the start and finish are positioned – competitions at a high level have been lost by competitors who have jumped a clear round and failed to go through the finish. It is important to go through the start looking towards the first fence and walking the line that will be taken to that fence: a good approach and a successful jump may set the standard for the rest of the course. From there on, the track to each fence must be walked exactly on the line that is going to be ridden. There is often a choice of track, one of which may reduce the time taken but make the approach to the fence more difficult. These alternatives must be studied, taking the horse's ability and experience into consideration.

Fences that are sited up to five strides apart are said to be at 'a related distance'. These should be paced out by the rider so that he knows exactly how many strides he will take between each fence – he must be able to decide whether his horse will do better to take four long strides or five shorter strides in, for example, a five-stride related distance that he feels is a bit short for his horse. The competition rider must be trained at home to measure the distances between fences by pacing them out. With experience he will be able to judge whether a related distance, or the distances in a double or combination fence, are going to be long or short for his horse.

Doubles and combinations are almost always set at 'true' distances, but the slope of the ground, the going and the siting of the fences may all affect the length of stride that the horse will take. The rider must take this into consideration when walking these obstacles – for instance he must be able to decide whether he should ride on because it is a longish double, or shorten up into a shortish double.

Course-builders sometimes site a perfectly fair fence where it will be knocked down by a careless or unbalanced horse or rider. For example this could be a stile out of a corner, or immediately fol-

lowing the water jump at which the horse will have had to gallop on. This problem will be noted by the astute competitor, and particular care taken on this part of the course.

In an attempt to make the course an interesting spectacle for the public, course-builders try to vary the colour and style of their jumps, frequently introducing new techniques. The competitor must note any particular colour or type of fence at which he may have had difficulty in training with his horse. Water trays, 'shark's teeth' planks and coloured fillers are all used to test the horse's courage and confidence; where they are new to the horse, and have perhaps not been seen before, they are a potential distraction and should be noted for careful and positive riding.

Walking the cross-country course

Meticulous walking of the cross-country course will reveal even more opportunities for saving time and energy than in a showjumping course. Time is invariably short in a cross-country competition and

• **Fig 140** Leading showjumpers walk the course at the Royal Show

all courses offer opportunities for saving – and wasting – time. The cross-country course is nearly always open for inspection the day before the competition, and is always open immediately before the competition starts; it can even be walked whilst the class is in progress. A plan of the course is always available.

The start and finish should be noted, although the finish is usually sited in such a way that competitors are automatically funnelled into it.

Careful walking of the track to be ridden is very important, as valuable seconds may be saved by avoiding rough, rutted or boggy ground: the shortest way is not necessarily the fastest as far as the going is concerned.

Each fence must be carefully studied to decide upon the approach and take-off area, the landing area, the angle at which the fence is to be jumped, the speed that is appropriate (an upright post-and-

LIBRARY
BISHOP BURTON COLLEGE
BEVERLEY HU17 8QG

TOM SMITH'S WALLS AT THE BADMINTON HORSE TRIALS

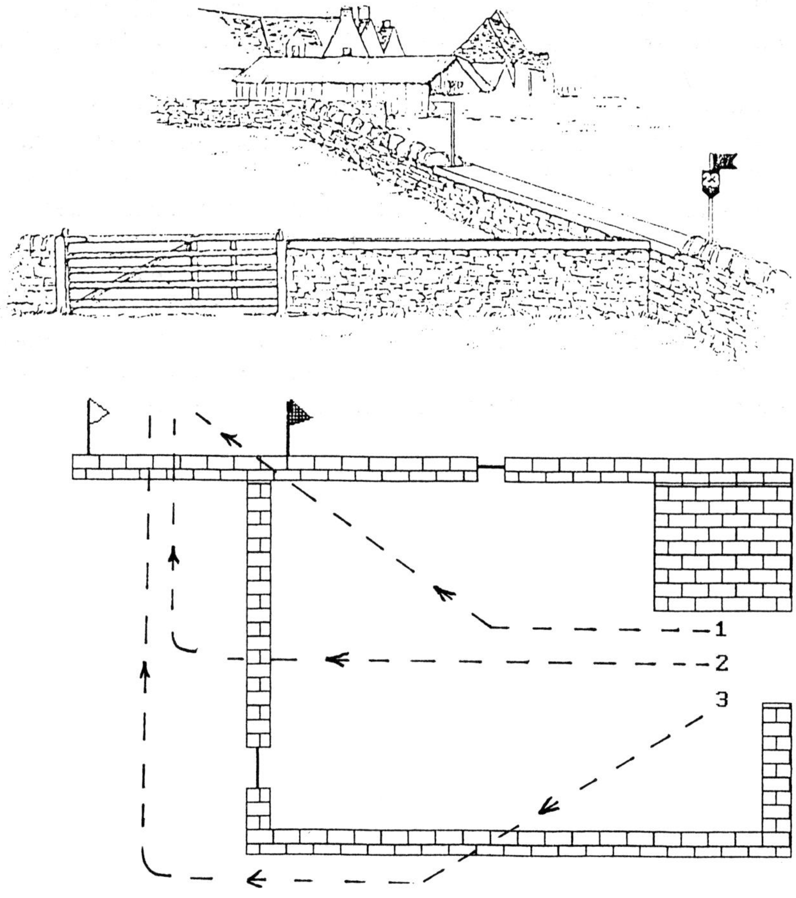

• **Fig 141** A typical cross-country fence with a choice of routes: Tom Smith's Walls at the Badminton Horse Trials **Route 1** is the shortest but involves jumping the corner

Route 2 is longer and involves jumping two walls **Route 3** is much longer, involves jumping two walls and a change of rein

rails with a drop on the landing side will not be jumped at the same speed as a plain steeplechase fence), the position of the next jump, and any alternatives that are offered. Added to this, consideration must be given as to whether the horse has seen this type of fence before – and if he has, whether or not it presented any particular problems.

Fences that include water need careful attention, with particular regard to the jump in, ie whether it is over a spread or an upright fence – an upright is easier as he may be able to trot into it; he may have to canter quite strongly into a spread. A different approach again is required if the jump has to be made out of water and into water. The depth of the water is important and should be checked by walking through it to assess the depth, and the quality of the going on the bottom. Nowadays longer stretches of water are being incorporated into cross-country courses, and these slow a horse down considerably. It is difficult to do more than a trot through water that is deeper than about 0.5m (18in). The retarding effect of landing in deep water is considerable and it is important to note where this may occur on the course.

Some fences will be set with alternative routes: the shorter route will be over bigger or more demanding fences, the longer route over less demanding fences. Whilst walking the course the rider must decide which route is best for his horse. Even if he decides to take the shorter route, he must study the alternative with equal care, lest he is compelled to use it because he fails in some way to follow his original plan (see Fig 141).

There will be areas on the course where he must go slowly and carefully, which will use up time; however, there will be others where he can gallop on and make up time. He should note these opportunities carefully to reduce the likelihood of incurring time penalties.

Some cross-country courses include 'obligatoires' (a pair of flags, red on the right and white on the left) through which competitors must pass. Failure to pass through these results in elimination, so they should be carefully noted.

The time of day and order of start may make a difference to the course. For example, at 4pm on a winter afternoon the sun may be very low, making a jump out of a dark wood into the sunlight a rather different obstacle to ride than it was at 10am the same day. In wet weather the muddy slope down to a fallen tree-trunk into the water will be much more slippery for the 40th horse than it was for the first few. There have been times when the cross-country course in major competitions has been entirely changed in character by a change of weather conditions during the event.

BITS, BITTING AND SCHOOLING DEVICES

BITTING THE COMPETITION HORSE

Ideally the competition horse, if correctly and progressively trained, should complete all his training up to medium dressage level in an ordinary snaffle bit. This Utopian aim is not unattainable and is often achieved. However, it would be unrealistic not to consider the circumstances in which, through faults in training, irregularities in conformation, problems in temperament, or a combination of two or more of these factors, some other type of bit should be considered in order that progress in training can be made.

In competition dressage the ordinary snaffle (together with a few limited variations) and the simple double bridle are the only permitted bits. Pelhams, gags, bitless bridles and other esoteric bits are forbidden by the rules, as is any type of martingale or balancing rein. Moreover these items of equipment are also prohibited whilst riding anywhere on the showground. For showjumping and cross-country riding the rules are more liberal, and gags, various pelhams, hackamore, and running martingales are frequently seen.

It is an old horseman's maxim that 'the bit is the key to the horse's mouth'. This may be so, but more important than the design of the bit is what the rider does with it once he is mounted and takes up the reins. Some bits are described as being more severe than others, but it is their 'potential for severe use' which is the most important consideration. A skilled horseman using a potentially severe bit can ride the horse calmly and without causing pain or distress. The unskilled horseman with a poor seat and rough hands has a potential for inflicting far more pain and damage with a severe bit than he would with perhaps a mild bit such as a straight rubber snaffle.

The bit should not be thought of as a mechanical device with which the horse can be physically controlled, but as a means of polite communication between rider and horse. In the best possible circumstances the horse learns to accept the bit surely and constantly on the bars of his mouth. To achieve this the rider must have a sufficiently well established seat, and a clear understanding of the purpose of the bit, to be able to keep a sure, steady, even contact through the reins and bit onto the horse's mouth. It is a popular thought in riding

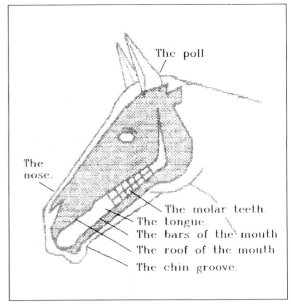

The poll

The nose.

The molar teeth.
The tongue.
The bars of the mouth
The roof of the mouth
The chin groove.

● **Fig 142** The areas on the horse's head on which the bit may have an effect

that the rein contact should be light. This is desirable, but a light rein with a contact that is continually varying is counter-productive, and does not encourage the horse to accept the bit. It is preferable to have a little more weight in the hand and be able to maintain a sure, steady, 'allowing' contact. The really skilled horseman is the one who can keep a steady, light contact.

The bit, when fitted with a noseband and some sort of martingale, has a potential for affecting various parts of the horse's head (see Fig 142). As the head plays an important role in balance and locomotion, any effect that the bit has on the head is likely to be reflected in other parts of the horse.

The aim is that the bit should act largely on the bars of the mouth which is the reason for working in the snaffle. Any bit which acts on the molar teeth, the roof of the mouth, the corners of the lips, the tongue, or is fitted so that it tends to cut off the air supply, is entirely unacceptable. However, there are occasions where a desirable effect can be obtained from a bit that puts pressure on the poll, the front of the nose or the chin groove, whilst acting at the same time on the bars of the mouth.

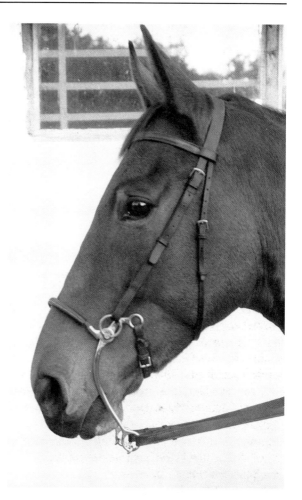

● **Fig 143** (right) The hackamore or bitless bridle

● **Fig 144** (below) The young horse working well in the snaffle and flash noseband

Snaffles

A jointed snaffle, working on the bars of the mouth, tends to encourage the horse to lower his head. When used in conjunction with a dropped, a flash or a grackle noseband, some pressure is put on the front of the nose and he is less able to escape from the action of the bit by opening his mouth too wide or crossing his jaw excessively. The snaffle bit is made in a variety of widths, from $4\frac{1}{2}$in for a 13hh pony, to $5\frac{1}{2}$in for a full-size hunter. This enables a bit of appropriate size to be fitted to most mouths. The joint creates a 'nutcracker' action on the lower jaw which may cause the horse some discomfort if carelessly used. If the bit is too wide and is used in conjunction with a noseband fitted below the bit, the joint may come into contact with the roof of the mouth, which is clearly unacceptable, particularly for the horse with a low soft pallet which is quite likely to be caused suffering. The 'nutcracker' action can be reduced to a degree by using a snaffle bit with two joints, or a 'French link' as it is sometimes known; and it can be removed altogether by using a straight-bar snaffle, or a 'mullen-mouth' snaffle, all of which are permitted under the rules of dressage. 'Eggbutt' snaffles reduce the risk of pinching the lips, and snaffle bits with various cheeks help to keep the bit steady in the mouth. These are all permitted in the dressage test up to advanced medium in pure dressage, and up to the FEI senior three-day event in horse trials, after which the double bridle is compulsory. In addition to these effects, the snaffle bridle exerts some pressure on the poll, particularly if used in conjunction with the running martingale.

The double bridle

It is most desirable if the horse can do all his work, up to that which requires advanced collection, in the snaffle bridle. The double bridle was once fashionable in the hunting field and was even used in conjunction with the running martingale, attached to the curb rein, as a means of increasing control. The purpose of the double bridle in true horsemanship is to enable the horse to be ridden on the bridoon (or snaffle) in most of his work, but to

• **Fig 145** Working well in the double bridle

be able to apply some pressure to the lower jaw, through the curb, as an aid to submission when greater impulsion and collection are required in advanced work. The action of the curb raises the head and flexes the lower jaw. Careful fitting is essential, particularly with regard to the adjustment of the curb chain. It should lie flat in the chin groove and, for normal working purposes, begin to come into effect when the action of the rein brings the Weymouth back to an angle of about 45°. However, sufficient time must be spent schooling in this bridle for both the horse and rider to be able to use it with confidence. From the rider it requires some dexterity in that he must ride with the normal contact on the bridoon, and keep sufficient contact on the curb to be able to use it when required, but *without* having it in constant use.

The double bridle is, as a rule, first introduced when the horse is working at elementary level and starting to work in collection. In the introductory stages it is fitted with the curb chain loose but not dangerously so, and little contact is taken on the curb rein. As his acceptance of the bridle and his confidence are established, the curb chain and curb rein can be gradually taken up until the Weymouth is having an effect. This introductory work is best introduced over a period of weeks rather than days. But, as in all horse training, precise timings can never be dogmatically laid down.

THE USE OF SPURS

The use of spurs is related to the use of the double bridle, so it is therefore appropriate to discuss their purpose here. At medium dressage level and for the dressage phase of an FEI senior three-day event their use is compulsory. Their purpose is to make the leg-aids more effective without the rider being encouraged to kick. When used in dressage they enable the rider, if he uses them correctly, to achieve greater activity from the horse's hind legs without excessive, inelegant use of the leg-aids. The type of spur chosen must be left to the trainer/ rider, but they should be sufficiently long to enable them to come into contact with the horse's sides without exaggerated turning of the rider's lower legs. A shorter spur is used for general training, showjumping and cross-country; again, its purpose is to make the leg-aids effective without kicking. In circumstances where the horse ignores the leg-

aid, it is usually counter-productive to kick harder as continued kicking may result in the horse becoming 'dead to the leg', which is undesirable. It is better that the correct leg-aid should be accompanied by a touch of the whip or use of the spur to achieve the desired response from the horse. Regulations covering the type of spurs permitted are included in the rules for a particular discipline.

Incorrect fitting of the spur detracts from its effectiveness. It should not be fitted loose, at the bottom of the heel, but high, at the top of the heel parallel to the ground. Only in this way can it be correctly and effectively used, without the risk of causing injury to the horse.

ARTIFICIAL SCHOOLING AIDS

There are a number of artificial schooling aids in general use which are intended to speed up training or overcome a particular difficulty. Their use is controversial, and has provided – and no doubt will continue to provide – a continual subject for discussion amongst practical horsemen.

In general, any item of equipment that compels or even encourages a horse to carry himself in a way for which he is neither physically nor mentally prepared will introduce a resistance, or a fault in some other aspect of his performance. When these items of equipment are used on a young, unspoiled horse as a short cut, or to compensate for lack of knowledge or skill on the part of the trainer, the horse's true potential must be inhibited. However, in the hands of an expert they may be useful in retraining a horse that has been spoilt by incorrect initial training, or to correct or relieve faults in conformation or action.

MARTINGALES

The running martingale

This simple device is widely used to prevent the horse from raising his head above the angle of control (see Fig 146). Even the most co-operative and obedient horses may, in the excitement of competition, tend to carry their heads undesirably high, and this is easily brought within controllable limits with the running martingale. It consists of a leather strap which is attached to the girth and passes between the horse's forelegs; it then passes through a neck-strap and divides into two, and at the end of

each of these branches a ring is fitted through which one rein passes. Each rein must be fitted with a martingale stop to prevent the ring from becoming hooked over the billet which attaches the rein to the bit. The neck-strap must be adjusted so that it allows a hand's breadth at the wither. The running martingale must be fitted sufficiently short to be effective, but not so short that it is always working and the rider is unable to relax it when it is not required. A useful guide to its length is that, when it is attached to the girth, the rings should just reach to the gullet. The most influential aspect of this martingale lies in the fact that it interrupts the direct feel between the rider's hands and the horse's mouth: passing the rein through a ring is similar to putting it through a pulley with the resulting reduction ratio that is incurred; thus rein-aids become more severe when passed through a running martingale ring.

• **Fig 146** The running martingale, used to prevent the horse from raising his head above the angle of control

The standing martingale

This is often used to improve rider control on a horse that tosses its head or consistently carries the head too high. It consists of a strap which attaches to the girth and is passed between the horse's forelegs; it then passes through the small loop on a neck-strap and attaches to the cavesson noseband. It must not be attached to a noseband that is fitted below the bit. To assess its correct length, when the martingale is fitted to both the girth and the noseband, and with the horse's head at a correct height, the martingale should just be able to be pushed up into the gullet. Remember that its use is prohibited under some competition rules.

NOSEBANDS

The dropped noseband

This noseband is fitted below the bit, and is intended to discourage the horse from opening his mouth too wide or from crossing his jaw. It is important that it is made to fit the horse for which it is intended, because the front of the noseband must be sufficiently long for it to remain well above the nostrils – it must never be fitted in a way that will restrict the breathing. The back of the noseband lies in the chin groove where it is adjusted to the appropriate length. Whilst it is fitted to discourage the horse from opening his mouth too wide, it must not be fitted so tight that he cannot open his mouth at all or flex his jaw. It is never used with a bit that incorporates a curb chain. It is often effectively used in conjunction with the 'Fulmer cheek' snaffle, where the lower cheeks on the bit help to keep the back part of the noseband in place, preventing it from slipping up – with a normal snaffle bit it could ride up over the bit-rings.

The 'flash' noseband

This is a cavesson noseband with a dropped noseband attached to the front of it. It is used for the same purposes as the dropped noseband and has two advantages: the first is that it is less likely that the dropped part of the flash noseband will be fitted too low, and the second is that it can be used with a standing martingale which the dropped noseband cannot.

The 'crossed' or 'grackle' noseband

This consists of two straps which cross in the front, then pass around the horse's jaws to join behind the mandible. Its purpose is the same as the dropped noseband but its action is spread over a larger area of the upper and lower jaws. Some horses accept the grackle more readily than the dropped noseband.

The 'Kineton' noseband

This incorporates the snaffle bit with the bitless bridle. On each side of the mouth a metal hook passes under the bit, behind the bit-ring; the hooks are joined across the front of the nose with an adjustable sort of dropped noseband. The whole device is supported by a bit head-stall. In circumstances where the horse pulls hard against the bit the noseband comes into effect rather like the noseband on a bitless bridle. Careful adjustment of the noseband is required to achieve the desired effect.

SCHOOLING DEVICES

The 'Chambon'

This is a French schooling device, used mainly on the lunge (see Figs 147 and 148). It consists of a strap from the girth which passes between the front legs and divides into two cords which pass through loops or pulleys on either side of a poll-pad, and pass down to be attached to the rings of the bit. The intention is that when the horse raises his head too high, the Chambon comes into effect, the bit pinches the corners of the mouth and pressure is put on the poll. To relieve this discomfort the horse lowers his head and neck, thereby taking the pressure off the poll and the corners of the mouth. Its advocates claim that it encourages the rounding of the back and the engagement of the hind legs. However, in the normal training of the horse he is encouraged to stretch his head and his neck forward and down to *seek* the bit and to *take* a contact. If the use of the Chambon encourages him to lower his head and neck in order to *escape* from the contact of the bit on the mouth, its action is contrary to the required effect. However, in expert hands it is often used to good effect in retraining spoilt or badly trained horses.

The 'de Gogue'

This is a variation of the Chambon, working on the same principle of putting pressure on the mouth and the poll when the head is carried high (see Figs 148, 149 and 152). It is more suitable for ridden work. It can be fitted in two ways: firstly, in the same way as the Chambon, although instead of being attached to the bit-rings the straps pass through the rings and join the main leather attachment. Or secondly, they pass through the bit-rings to the rider where they are held like reins. Its adherents claim that, like the Chambon, the de Gogue encourages submission, a rounder back, and engagement of the hind legs. It is a device which the serious trainer/rider should study, and then he can draw his own conclusions as to whether or not there is a place for this equipment, with some horses, in practical horsemanship.

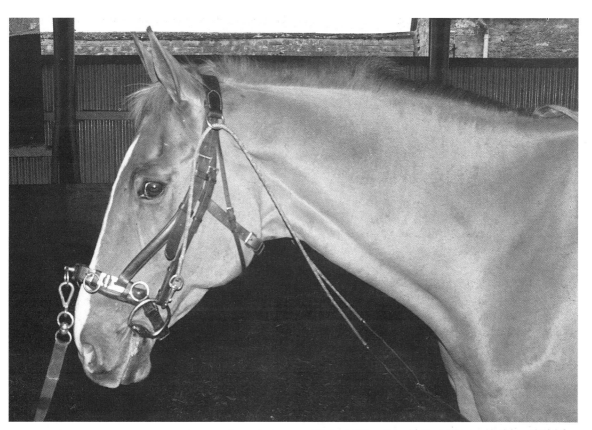

Fig 147 The Chambon correctly fitted

Fig 148 The Chambon in action: many horses work with a lowered head and neck position and rounded topline just from the feel of the Chambon in position

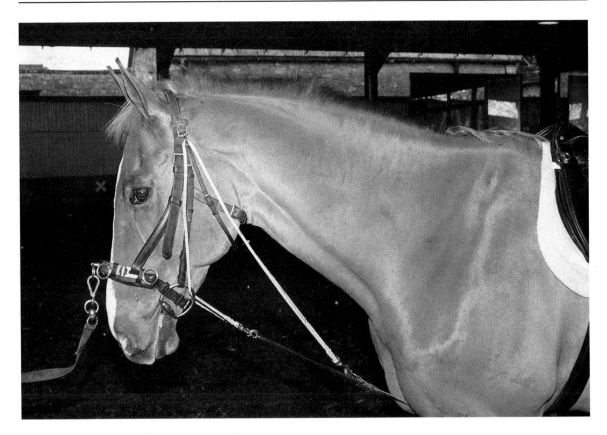

● **Fig 149** The de Gogue fixe fitted for lungeing

● **Fig 150** Lungeing on the de Gogue fixe

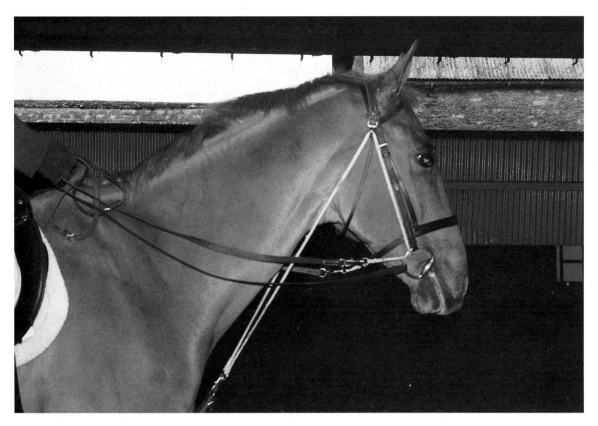

Fig 151 The de Gogue fitted 'commandez'

Fig 152 The de Gogue ridden 'commandez'

'Draw-reins'

These are reins that start at the centre of the girth and pass between the forelegs, up through the rings of the bit to the rider's hands where they join. Fitted in this way they have a very severe action, since they compel the horse's head to come down and to a certain extent back. Inexpertly used they can cause severe overbending, which is a serious fault; or they cause the horse to come behind the bit, a fault which once established is very difficult to correct.

● **Fig 153** Correct use of the draw reins

Alternatively, the draw-reins can be attached to the girth by the buckles on either side; then – as before – they pass through the bit-rings to the rider's hands where they join. This method of fitting clearly increases the backward pull on the jaw, and is obviously undesirable. Draw-reins are used by many advanced trainers/riders in schooling and warming up for competitions where the horse is known to be inattentive and slow to settle to his work. In these circumstances they are acceptable in expert hands. But in the hands of the inexperienced, where they are used to pull the unschooled horse's head down, their potential for causing lasting damage and problems is considerable.

● **Fig 154** Last minute checks in the box before Phase D; Tanya Cleverley and Watkins at the Badminton Horse Trials

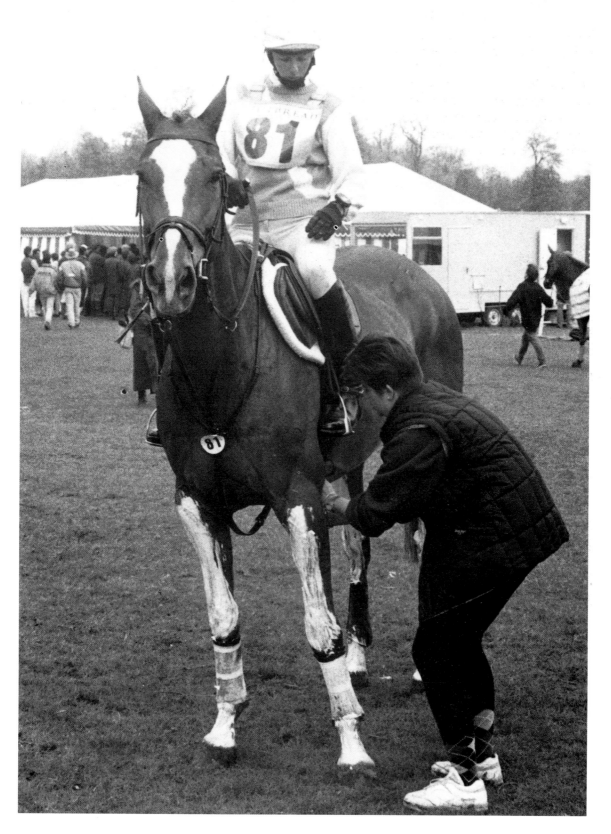

EQUESTRIAN TITLES FROM DAVID & CHARLES

A PHOTOGRAPHIC GUIDE TO STABLE MANAGEMENT	Robert Oliver
BEHAVIOUR PROBLEMS IN HORSES	Susan McBane
COMPETITION TRAINING For Horse and Rider	Monty Mortimer
DAVID BROOME'S TRAINING MANUAL	Marcy Pavord
FITNESS FOR HORSE AND RIDER	Jane Holderness-Roddam
FROM FOAL TO FULL-GROWN	Janet Lorch
HORSE BREEDING	Peter Rossdale
HORSE CARE & RIDING A Thinking Approach	Susan McBane
KEEPING A HORSE OUTDOORS	Susan McBane
LUNGEING The Horse & Rider	Sheila Inderwick
MARY THOMSON'S EVENTING YEAR A Month-by-Month Plan for Training a Champion	Debby Sly with Mary Thomson
PRACTICAL DRESSAGE	Jane Kidd
PRACTICAL EVENTING	Jane Holderness-Roddam
PRACTICAL SHOWING	Nigel Hollings
PRACTICAL SHOWJUMPING	Peter Churchill
ROBERT SMITH'S YOUNG SHOWJUMPER Selecting, Training, Competing	Rachel Lambert
THE HORSE OWNER'S HANDBOOK	Monty Mortimer
THE HORSE RIDER'S HANDBOOK	Monty Mortimer
THE HORSE'S HEALTH FROM A TO Z An Equine Veterinary Dictionary	Peter Rossdale & Susan Wreford
THE ILLUSTRATED GUIDE TO HORSE TACK	Susan McBane
THE LESS-THAN-PERFECT RIDER Overcoming Common Riding Problems	Lesley Bayley & Caroline Davis
THE RIDING INSTRUCTOR'S HANDBOOK	Monty Mortimer
THE STABLE VETERINARY HANDBOOK	Colin Vogel
UNDERSTANDING HORSE'S The Key to Success	Garda Langley

INDEX

● **Fig 155** A good first impression is essential for success in competition

Fig 156 Jumping into the water at Gatcombe Park